Crossing Borders, Sharing Burdens

Lotta Björklund Larsen • Lynne Oats

Crossing Borders, Sharing Burdens

Rethinking Taxation and Migration as Fiscal Belonging

palgrave
macmillan

Lotta Björklund Larsen
University of Galway
Galway, Ireland

Lynne Oats
University of Exeter
Exeter, UK

ISBN 978-3-031-99393-0 ISBN 978-3-031-99394-7 (eBook)
https://doi.org/10.1007/978-3-031-99394-7

This work was supported by University of Exeter

This Palgrave Macmillan imprint is published by the registered company Springer Nature Switzerland AG
The registered company address is: Gewerbestrasse 11, 6330 Cham, Switzerland

Preface

Tax matters. Its impact on people and societies is enormous but also changing. It is important to remember that tax does not happen in a national bubble but is affected by a variety of global shifts. For example, heightened concerns about the impact of climate change has moved debates on from broad environmental concerns to a focus on global warming leading to the introduction of net zero targets. This has led to a reappraisal of environmental regulation measures, including taxes. Demographic shifts also have implications for tax systems. There are three particular demographic trends: population growth,[1] which is expected to continue over the next 50–60 years; population ageing, such that it is estimated that by 2080 persons over 65 years of age will outnumber children under 18; and international migration which obviously reduces populations in some areas but increases populations in others. All of these shifts will have implications for tax policy.

Digitalisation is already having profound effects on societies across the globe. It has changed the way business and governments operate and created opportunities for new markets to emerge. For example, we have moved from relatively simple data analytics to generative artificial intelligence. Material goods are increasingly being replaced by intellectual property. Even assets such as cryptocurrency and non-fungible tokens are now residing in cyber space. Digitalisation affects not only *what* we tax but

[1] According to the United Nations, see https://population.un.org/wpp/assets/Files/WPP2024_Key-Messages.pdf

how we tax, providing tax administrations with new ways of monitoring and managing compliance with tax rules.

Last but not least in this Preface, we recognise that geopolitics is changing the way in which countries interact with each other, which also has implications for the way national tax systems are designed and international tax operates. Russia's invasion of Ukraine has interrupted supply chains and energy supplies. The American policy move towards increasing use of tariffs challenges people's role in society. Global trade has shifted from protectionism to cooperation and is now shifting back to protectionism with tax at the heart of it.

These are all potent examples of trends that affect, and are affected by, tax systems and tax policy. With the profound changes going on in the world, we find it a good time to discuss how we understand tax.

This book builds on fieldwork that took place in the second half of 2021 and early 2022. What a quiet time it now seems authoring this book in spring 2025. All we had to deal with at the time was a global pandemic and its aftermath. Some of the trends noted above were on the horizon but somehow seemed less pressing; some were outright unimaginable.

Tax as an object of study is of interest not only to a wide range of academic disciplines but also to all tax experts, who deal with taxation in practice every day—in small and large businesses, in tax consultancies or in tax collecting administrations. Yet, what concerns do we have regarding tax? Why do people pay tax, why do they not pay tax and how are they made to pay tax? Do our concerns relate to strict legal interpretation, or rules and regulations created by tax administrations? Or are we concerned about recommendations by tax advisers or perhaps the economic impact certain types of tax will have made? These are just a few of many questions around tax. If we have questions and concerns, we also want answers. A relevant question is thus: what does tax knowledge consist of, what premises underlie it, but also who has created such knowledge and how?

Our own research, individually and together, adopts ethnographic methods and perspectives to probe tax issues as encountered and discussed by our participants. In this book we introduce you to a number of theoretical perspectives from the social sciences that rely on qualitative material and interpretative analysis. We want to illustrate other forms of tax knowledge. The privileging of mountainous quantified knowledge has largely kept qualitative insights in the shadows. To illustrate the value of qualitative approaches, in this book we draw in particular on our participation in a funded research project entitled 'Fiscal Citizenship in Migrant Societies'.

The project was funded by the Open Research Area, a joint initiative between the research funding councils of five countries. Funding was applied for in September 2019, in the heady days before the global pandemic, when a multidisciplinary consortium of researchers from the UK, Canada and Germany was established. By the time the project started, in March 2021, the pandemic was still rumbling on. Why 'fiscal citizenship'? We decided the term best captured what we were trying to analyse, a term used by several authors, as we discuss in Chap. 2, but not usually defined with any specificity. We spent considerable time—virtually, due to travel restrictions—thinking about the scope of fiscal citizenship and refining a work plan consisting of related studies using a variety of research methods. We are grateful to all colleagues participating in the 'Fiscal Citizenship' team (in Canada, Germany and the UK)—to their work, engagement and discussions that have also helped shape this book.

Most of our colleagues engaged in studies coalescing around a positivist approach and quantitative methods. Our work took a different approach being both interpretivist (with a critical edge) and qualitative, and this book is the culmination of our endeavours to listen to immigrants in the UK and think carefully about what they told us.

We make four contributions:

- Critical perspective: a critical perspective allows us to probe more deeply and challenge entrenched positions in our collective understanding of the role of taxation in society.
- Fiscal belonging: we develop a new, multifaceted, concept that sits alongside fiscal citizenship but places the emphasis on social relations between migrants and the state, and between fellow members of society. belonging
- Thick and thin reciprocity: we nuance received understandings of reciprocity as being tit for tat, highlighting the complexity of feelings of reciprocity.
- Fiscal culture: our concept of fiscal culture moves us beyond simplistic categorisations and underscores the importance of a holistic view, taking into account not only contributions to the state in the form of taxes, but also what we receive from the state in the form of benefits.

Organisation of the Book

Chapter 1 introduces the topography of tax. A map metaphor is often found when discussing epistemology in the social sciences; we build on this and use topography as a way to sketch how the academic disciplines take tax as an object of study. Compared to a map, a topography better recognises the materiality of a landscape and visualises it as three-dimensional. Thinking with a topography allows us to see how each discipline has its own identity, norms and connections with, but also autonomy from, other disciplines and preferred methods of inquiry although we are all interested in the same topic—taxation.

Disciplines are important in structuring how we think about tax, not only for researchers working within them in academic institutions, but also for those working in 'the wild'. By thinking with topography we aim to challenge all those interested in tax including tax professionals regardless of which academic discipline within which they have received training. It is not only the public that concentrates on the political viewpoint of the originator. We find it of vital importance to appreciate the epistemological premises underlying any survey and report; to ask *how* has a specific report generated the conclusions made? What assumptions underlie the conclusions, and what proxies are used to simplify difficult concepts? What traps do we need to be aware of when reading scholarly tax research?

In Chap. 2, we reflect on both fiscal citizenship and fiscal belonging conceptually, by reference to other scholars who have tried to understand and describe the phenomena. The term 'fiscal citizenship' is often used to describe the relationship people have to the state through paying taxes and the ensuing relationships: between citizen and state and between fellow citizens. The concept of fiscal citizenship appears to derive largely from American scholarship, perhaps as there the notion of citizenship is strongly correlated with the duty of submitting information about tax, indeed jurisdiction to tax is much more closely entwined with citizenship in the USA than in other countries. Importantly, however, citizenship was not a topic that animated our participants when they spoke about taxes and taxation—the impact on themselves, on people broadly and on societies they have lived in. The chapter also describes our methodology: our fieldwork, our participants and the ensuing material and analysis methods. We finish the chapter by presenting our critical social science approach to tax research.

Chapter 3 describes the context our participants find themselves in and the realities they relate to when thinking about tax, talking about tax and conducting tax-related work. The focus of the chapter is to briefly describe how people navigate the UK fiscal field. *Fiscal belonging* in the British context encompasses the collection of revenue by government in the form of taxes, but importantly also governmental spending in the provision of services to society. But as we engaged with immigrants to the UK, it became clear they also have to deal with practical migration issues while adapting to British society. Four citizenship controversies end the chapter. These happened over the last decade and were referred to by our participants. These controversies remind us that the complexity of taxation impacts many aspects of life but also underlines that people constantly change their views on taxation.

Chapter 4 draws on the ethnographic fieldwork conducted in the Fiscal Citizenship project. Of particular interest in this is the situation of migrants. Fiscal citizenship might be more difficult to articulate for migrants that have arrived in a country for many reasons: for work, fleeing war, staying on after completing an education, for love, etc. Migrants may even have contributed to their adopted society by paying taxes for a long, long time yet have not been classed as citizens. We see a need to expand our understanding of citizenship beyond the formal/legal domain to better conceptualise fiscal citizenship. To further this aim, drawing on the stories of migrants, we show how the notion of belonging is articulated in relation to tax and citizenship. Inspired by Nira Yuval-Davis' facets of belonging, we propose four facets of fiscal belonging: *work, family, (social) acceptance* and *(political and cultural) values.*

Chapter 5 describes in detail how we see the third point of our contribution. We explore how the concept of reciprocity enriches our understanding of taxation beyond its traditional definition as a compulsory, unrequited payment as often offered by textbooks and dictionaries. It aims to take seriously the many sentiments people express that in essence mean 'getting something for your money'. Yet, as we will show, there is seldom a simple tit-for-tat reasoning underlying this sentiment. We thus introduce thin and thick reciprocity to nuance, but also bringing depth and flesh, to the four facets of fiscal belonging. While what we refer to as thin reciprocity may dominate policy models and compliance research due to its measurability, we argue that thick reciprocity, which is harder to quantify, provides essential insights into civic solidarity, identity and moral engagement with the state.

In Chap. 6 we take a broader approach, also inspired by the reflections of our participants, and describe the concept of *fiscal culture* from a critical perspective, as our fourth contribution. Fiscal culture provides an overarching approach to understanding how people see the connection between taxes collected and public expenses. The concept of fiscal culture underlines how taxpayer behaviour is seldom described by static categories such as nationality, country of origin, being native or an immigrant, gender, etc. Instead, it allows us to provide a more holistic perspective and see how they relate to both paying taxes and receiving benefits from them. In order to propose a fiscal culture, we will first review some important work on one side of it—that of tax culture. We then move on to exemplify with a few important anthropological studies the notion of culture—culture being one of the most central, and disputed, concepts in anthropological research. Applying an anthropological perspective allows us to take a more holistic view of fiscal culture. We end the chapter by looking at how fiscal culture can be applied to Paulina's narrative, born and educated in Bolivia and now working as a human rights lawyer in London.

In Chap. 7 we conclude, proposing some insights that our approach to the topography of taxation may provide but also look into the unforeseeable future. We do not know what it will bring except that we are certain that there will be changes. We already know about generative AI, climate change, demographic changes and geopolitical upheaval, including emerging trade wars precipitated by tax in the form of tariffs, but there might even be black swans in our landscape. The question is how will people react to new taxes and ways to tax. What will they do to society?

Galway, Ireland — Lotta Björklund Larsen
Exeter, UK — Lynne Oats

Acknowledgements

This is a book which is both very short and long in the making. The perspective we propose is based on research into the intriguing world of tax over many years. We are particularly grateful to our research participants who generously shared their views on what is often considered to be a very private matter, at a time when we were all emerging from the horror of the global pandemic.

We are most grateful to our colleagues in the Fiscal Citizenship team for both challenging and encouraging us: Jonathan Farrar, Martin Fochmann, Till-Arne Hahn, Oliver James, Dirk Kiesewetter, Hans-Joachim Lauth, Eva Matthei, Clare Maudling, Ralf Schenke, Charlotte Schmidt, Kim-Lee Tuxhorn and Josef Wunderlich. Our thanks also go to Hans Gribnau, John d'Attoma, Miranda Sheild Johansson and Ulf Hannerz for both inspirational and helpful comments. As always, many thanks to Pat Baxter for her diligent language editing.

The Fiscal Citizenship project was funded by three funding bodies under the auspices of the Open Area Research programme: Economic and Social Research Council (UK) Grant Ref ES/V013572/1, Deutsche Forschungsgemeinschaft (DFG, German Research Foundation)–Projektnummer 440793159 and Social Sciences and Humanities Research Council (Canada) Grant Ref 2004–2020-0008.

Open access funding was generously provided by UKRI.

About the Book

Tax matters. It structures our societies, influences our choices, and reflects our values. Yet the meaning and impact of taxation are constantly changing in step with a world marked by climate transitions, demographic shifts, digitalisation, globalisation, and migration.

This open access book addresses critical questions surrounding attitudes to tax and tax compliance through the lens of 'fiscal belonging', demonstrating the value of qualitative approaches to tax research. It explores the lived experience of immigrants to the UK, and how feelings of belonging, exclusion, reciprocity, and obligation shape their encounters with the tax system. The book illuminates the many different facets of fiscal belonging, including the right to work and access to employment, as well as histories of colonialism and the economic history of different communities on a national scale. By foregrounding personal narratives and the complexity of social worlds, this book argues for more methodologically diverse and inclusive approaches to understanding why people do, or do not, pay tax. It will be of interest to scholars across disciplines, as well as tax professionals working in business, consultancy, and public administration.

Contents

Notes on Contributors

Lotta Björklund Larsen is Adjunct Professor at University of Galway and holds a PhD in Social Anthropology from Stockholm University. 'Why we pay tax, why we avoid doing so and how we are made to pay tax' are questions that illuminate people's relation to state, community and fellow citizens. She is convinced of the need for a multidisciplinary approach to the tax field if we are to understand the intriguingly complex issue of taxation and how it affects people in everyday life.

Through ethnographic engagement with diverse stakeholders in the tax arena, she has examined the epistemologies shaping tax compliance, the making of a tax gap, informal economies, tax lotteries and the digitisation of tax systems. Her research has resulted in numerous peer-reviewed articles and monographs: *A Fair Share of Tax: A Fiscal Anthropology of Contemporary Sweden* (2018, Palgrave Macmillan) and *Shaping Taxpayers: Values in Action at the Swedish Tax Agency* (2017, Berghahn Books). Lotta has received numerous research grants and served as co-investigator on the project Fiscal Citizenship.

Lynne Oats is Emeritus Professor of Taxation, University of Exeter. Her research interests centre on taxation as a social and institutional practice, embracing historical and contemporary tax policy both nationally and internationally. She constantly pushes back against the confines of the academic discipline in which she has been placed and has published numerous journal articles and book chapters across a wide span of subjects, with collaborators from a range of disciplinary backgrounds. Her books include *Taxation Policy and Practice*, *Principles of International Taxation* and *Taxation: A Fieldwork Research Handbook.*

Lynne Oats has been involved in several funded research projects including the Tax Administration Research Centre and most recently was Principal Investigator on the Fiscal Citizenship project which funded this book.

CHAPTER 1

A Topography of Tax Knowledge

Abstract This chapter addresses tax knowledge, where it comes from and how it is used and understood. Scholarly tax knowledge, as distinct from the tax knowledge of laypersons, varies in many ways, the premises on which it is based, the prior knowledge that is built upon, how it is used by other scholars and in practice by policymakers and others. We describe scholarly tax knowledge in topographical terms, to highlight the distinctions between academic disciplines. We also point to some areas where traps await the unwary, who may not be fully aware of the underlying assumptions and special language used within particular disciplines. Finally, we describe our own approach to generating tax knowledge, using ethnographic methods, an interpretive approach and a critical eye.

Keywords Tax knowledge • Positivism • Interpretivism • Qualitative and quantitative methods • Academic disciplines

This book is about travellers. The participants in our study are all immigrants to Britain, who travelled here for varying reasons, some of whom stayed and some of whom left. We wanted to understand how they interact with the tax system, how they gain tax knowledge and how they feel about paying taxes. In this chapter we describe how we approach tax research.

L. Björklund Larsen, L. Oats, *Crossing Borders, Sharing Burdens*,
https://doi.org/10.1007/978-3-031-99394-7_1

But it is not only immigrants that travel through the tax landscape. All who engage with tax issues encounter the results of various approaches to tax: the results of researching tax and curating tax knowledge.

What is tax knowledge? It is both a broad and a diffuse term. Most people in the world are in one way or another affected by tax and have an opinion on the subject. Such knowledge is the result of diffusion through society. Much of it originates in academic scholarship, encyclopaedia and textbook definitions and is applied by think tanks, governmental institutions and while collecting taxes. Tax knowledge consists of the facts, skills, truths and insights that a person may apply in theory and in practice when dealing with tax. In this chapter we are not concerned, however, with the tax knowledge of our participants—that will come in later chapters. Here we are concerned with *scholarly* tax knowledge, as a backdrop to our methodology.

Our study started, as most do, with looking at what has already been found out by other scholars, paying careful attention to *how* their findings were generated. Readers will find reference to the literature that we found to be most useful throughout the book.

How then do tax *scholars* acquire knowledge? Epistemology is the theory of knowledge: what can we know and how we can find out about it? A map metaphor is often found when discussing epistemology in the social sciences. Cèline-Marie Pascale, for example, suggests that 'the use of cartography as a metaphor alludes to geographies of power expressed in technologies for generating knowledge' (2011, p. 1). The idea of mapping the disparate approaches to tax had some appeal for us, but we wondered if it could fully capture the many different ways of thinking and talking about tax. This led us to muse about topography, and how it could be used to better understand one particular form of tax knowledge: scholarly tax knowledge. In addition to the volume of tax knowledge, there are also differences in the content of tax knowledge which is precisely the point we want to make with our topography. We believe topography gives us greater purchase on understanding the myriad ways in which scholars and others think and talk about tax. Topographical metaphors draw attention to the vast and varied landscape that is tax knowledge and allow us to reflect on relations between the different forms of knowledge we engage with. Compared to a map, topography better recognises the materiality of a landscape. Topography visualises the three dimensions of a landscape. It pays attention to the various landforms, such as mountains, hills, plains and plateaus. Lakes, streams, soils (such as sand or clay) and natural vegetation are other features that are more distinct in topography than on a map. It is well recognised that tax is obscenely complex (e.g. Clemens, 1999), which provides a barrier to entry for all, as well as a barrier to interdisciplinary conversations among scholars to advance tax knowledge (Björklund Larsen & Lauth, 2025). This is where topography proves to be a helpful concept to think with; a three-dimensional perspective noting its materiality makes it easier to make our way through the landscape.

Tax Knowledge

There are many different types of knowledge and ways of categorising it, but for our purpose we make the distinction between explicit, implicit, theoretical and practical knowledge.

Explicit knowledge is factual and can easily be written down or explained: when the tax return is due, who administers tax payments, how tax payments are made, what percentage you pay in tax and more. Tax professionals, both advisers and tax inspectors, obviously have enormous amounts of explicit knowledge, often blending various elements of the topography. Taxpayers may not have explicit knowledge, relying on advisers to guide them.

Implicit or tacit knowledge comprises skills or understandings of tax that are harder to articulate. You know you have to pay tax but are not entirely sure on what? This can lead to everyday avoidance strategies such as how to conduct work and be paid informally. Such arrangements are often based on sensing someone's mood or interpreting a social situation.

Theoretical knowledge is the understanding of why something is the way it is. For a legal scholar this can be an understanding why the tax law is constructed in certain ways, for a historian how the tax systems has evolved over time, for a sociologist how taxation makes an impact (beyond the economic) on the lives for certain categories of people or wider society.

Practical knowledge. This is knowing how to deal with taxation in everyday life. For a person with low income living in the UK tax is most often hidden as they are below the threshold for paying income tax and that VAT is often overlooked in everyday purchases. For an accountant, the practical knowledge of tax makes up a large part of the daily workload.

At its core, tax knowledge is the combination of information, context and the ability to apply it. It might seem that scholarly tax knowledge is distant from that of laypersons trying to make sense of their obligations, indeed that they are completely disconnected. But scholarly tax knowledge permeates understandings of tax, and especially tax compliance, throughout society. Yet it is often hard to discern.

Attempts to generate knowledge about tax also raise methodological challenges within and outside of academia resulting in compromises and contradictions, yet particular methods and certain ways of thinking have become dominant. This creates hierarchies of knowledge in which certain perspectives and methods become the most visible part of the landscape, leaving alternative perspectives hidden or forgotten in more secluded valleys. This is unfortunate. In what follows we sketch a new way of thinking about *scholarly* tax knowledge. We do not seek to be prescriptive but rather aim to open up new conversations and to throw down a challenge to entrenched ways of thinking about and doing tax research.

The Academic Disciplines as Landscape

We start with a sketch, possibly a caricature, of the academic disciplines that take tax as an object of study. We acknowledge the crudeness of our depictions, and we ask readers for indulgence, but sometimes the complexity of the different approaches of academic disciplines is not fully appreciated, and so our aim is to draw attention to this. We don't seek to be comprehensive here and only cover a selection of disciplines for illustrative purposes. Each of these disciplines has its own identity, norms, connections with, but also autonomy from, other disciplines and preferred methods of inquiry and analysis. We also acknowledge that academic disciplines are artificial constructs and are not necessarily constituted in the same way across the globe (Oats et al., 2025). Nonetheless, they are important in structuring how we think about tax, not only for researchers working within them in academic institutions, but also for those 'in the wild', the real world. We thus want to challenge all those who may have received prior training in one or more academic disciplines and then found their way into think tanks, non-governmental organisations (NGOs), policymaking, the media, private tax advisory roles and other positions of influence. But for any person interested in tax and taxation, the epistemological premises underlying both education curricula and academic research are important to understand, as well as the results of surveys and reports addressing tax issues. Often, the public concentrates on the simple political viewpoint of the originator; left or right, more or less tax, which tax? We want to direct your focus to ask *on what premises* a specific document—report, book, article—has generated the eventual conclusions?

Philosophers

The discipline of philosophy can be thought of as mountain ranges, to some extent detached but with an expansive outlook. Taking a bird's eye view, perched atop the mountains, we find some, but not many, philosophers and theologians contemplating the world of tax. Their insights provide us with a moral foundation for tax (van Brederode, 2022). Philosophers are concerned with the totality of the landscape, the innate reasons for paying tax—or not paying it. This is frequently overlooked or at least overshadowed by legal and economic viewpoints that have more practical application. Philosophers are the conscience of the landscape, concerned with morals, ethics and overall meaning, but at an abstract level. Sometimes there is engagement with the actual details of the landscape, but it is an aesthetic view, where parts of the landscape make up a more or less pleasing outlook—and thus looks towards our moral conscience.

Historians

History can be thought of as the bedrock of our disciplinary topography. All disciplinary spaces have a history that may or may not be well known. The history of contemporary tax issues is often obscured by layers of urban development and vegetation. Historians are the archaeologists, clearing away the accumulation of sedimented events, delving into the archives to discover antecedents, shifts and possible lessons for the present. When we know how something comes to be, through historical analysis, and we know how things are now, we have a means to think about how things will develop in the future (Brinkmann et al., 2020).

Legal and Accounting Scholars

The discipline of law is largely autonomous from other disciplines and is generally well structured, although the relative status of tax law within the wider body of legal scholarship varies from country to country. Thinking about tax as a legal phenomenon is a bit like entering an urban area. We find structures and roads, although not always well designed, with signposts that may or may not be clear. Nonetheless, there is an air of order about tax law, and it has the backing of a legal framework that aims to provide protection from arbitrary decisions, for example, of tax authorities, and ways of resolving disagreements. A legal approach to tax, however, is highly specialised and often insulated from social concerns and political influences.

Legal scholars are concerned with the directions, signposts, indication of places and distances—of directing us where to go and how to get there. There are traffic signs indicating bumpy roads and sharp turns. Prohibitive signs, signs giving orders, positive instructions, information and warning signs. Tax law tells us what to do, what is prohibited and sometimes also what will happen if you do/don't do it. Lawyers read and write signs and are concerned that signposting is appropriate and correct.

The discipline of accounting is compatible with law in that accountants in tax are also concerned with the signs, helping their clients navigate their complexity and mediating between client and the state in terms of compliance with tax laws. In so doing, they are interested in yields and measurements. Accounting scholarship is heavily influenced by economics and within the accounting discipline tax is mainly thought of as an economic phenomenon. There are also accounting scholars who study why taxpayers avoid the signs altogether—the deviations from tax compliance which bring us to tax avoidance and evasion.

Political Scientists

The discipline of political science runs through the fiscal world like roads, highways, rural tracks and mountain passes. Political scientists are especially concerned with how states are governed and how different political institutions constrain or enable the development of laws and regulations. What roles do public administrations take and how do they exercise their power? Political scientists rummage through the landscape and aim to understand how the different geographic features interrelate but also how they can be changed and what the implications will be. What will be the consequences for the landscape if we change the course of a stream? Applied to tax, how would a nation's welfare institutions change if, for example, wealth is taxed—or not taxed?

Economists

The discipline of economics is pervasive in the tax landscape; maybe we can think of it as the variety of vegetation that can be found throughout. It is more verdant in some areas than others and especially in fields, farmland and meadows. Economics is concerned with efficiency and thus about measurement: the production, distribution and consumption of goods and services and the behaviours and decisions associated with these processes. Economics is abstract and so is our understanding of its place in our topographic model of the tax landscape. Economic models consist of formulas with different variables. Economic models always assume a standpoint from which the formula/model relates to other issues. Depending on standpoint, the result may change. At a very simplified level, we see economists as surveyors, measuring relations; it can be between two, perhaps several, different points in the landscape or comparing the yields between certain fields or forests.

As a sub-discipline of economics, behavioural economics is flourishing amid a general upsurge in behavioural 'science', a common thread across the disciplines discussed in the next section. It borrows methods from other social sciences and is based on the assumption that 'increasing the realism with which individual behaviour is seen will improve the ability to predict behaviour and devise appropriate policies' (Alm & Kasper, 2022, p. 1). Behavioural economists systematically explore a carefully cultivated landscape to understand the minds of its inhabitants.

Anthropologists and Sociologists

The academic disciplines of anthropology and sociology are related in their interest in the functioning of societies, much like the forests and gardens that are the lungs of the planet. Like philosophers, anthropologists and sociologists are also concerned with an overall perspective, yet engaging with describing and understanding the relations between objects in the landscape. What are the different components in the landscape, what is their purpose and how do they relate to one another? Just as some vegetation thrives on a particular soil, anthropologists describe tax behaviours 'in the wild' and thus aim to discern any discrepancies between morals, written laws and regulations, and actual practices. Anthropologists as foresters cannot do much about the landscape they travel through, but they question why people do not follow the signs. If anthropologists are foresters, sociologists are gardeners. They study the structure, interaction and collective behaviour of specified groups or categories of human beings. Sociologists often propose certain taxes or tax systems out of specific concerns for certain categories of people. They have a plan for how the landscape will look. Sociologists begin with their assumptions about the actual relations between different categories and often want to change them; they want to structure nature and make an accessible park or garden.

Travellers Passing Through

Finding the way through this landscape looking at a map might be a challenge, if not outright confusing. Yet, throughout the disciplinary landscape we sketch above there can be found common threads which make it easier for the traveller to grapple with several aspects of it. Each disciplinary space has a mainstream or dominant way of thinking about what matters and how best to study it. This mainstream is usually entrenched and carefully guarded by gatekeepers, for example, senior academics and journal editors. In each of the disciplines we describe above, positivism, which we discuss in more detail in the next section, tends to dominate in most disciplines, as does quantification.

Behaviouralism[1] tries to explain observable human behaviour and has grown in importance in recent decades in a number of disciplines, not only in the social sciences but also in the natural sciences. Indeed we now speak of behavioural sciences, echoing the efforts of economics to emulate the physical sciences in seeking universal laws, craving generalisability, that every city can be comparable. This is most prevalent in economic psychology—after all, psychology has always been concerned with behaviour. Joined with economics in the form of economic psychology, behavioural science has become a powerful mechanism for explaining tax compliance or non-compliance, for example. Behaviouralism has led to an influential movement, behavioural insights, which promulgates 'nudge' techniques aimed at modifying people's behaviour. Nudge is popular in many tax authorities as an apparently easy approach to encouraging tax compliance, albeit sometimes overlooking ethical concerns.[2]

The hegemonic presence of positivism and quantification overshadows other forms of knowledge and knowledge generation. In most disciplinary spaces, with important exceptions such as anthropology, interpretivism is

[1] As distinct from behaviourism which seeks to condition behaviour as exemplified by the work of psychologist B.F. Skinner.

[2] For example, see the 2019 OECD public consultation document *Tax Morale: What Drives People and Businesses to Pay Tax?* Available at https://www.oecd.org/en/publications/2019/09/tax-morale_8d593d89.html

marginalised as unscientific. Similarly, mastery of qualitative methods is often viewed as inferior and qualitative data often dismissed as anecdotal.

The final common thread, albeit a more fragile one, is critical scholarship. In each of the disciplinary spaces there can be found scholars who push back against the mainstream, calling into question the received wisdom of those seeking to stand alongside the sciences dealing with the physical world. In ancient maps, unknown spaces were labelled 'there be dragons'. Critical scholarship is often viewed as alien, strange, on the outskirts and even draconic. Certainly, the number of scholars who describe themselves as critical is much smaller than those in the mainstream. Yet there are different strands of critical scholarship. Some identify flaws in practices, maybe seeking radical change. Others draw on social theories or perspectives from outside of their home discipline to question and reinterpret received views (Oats et al., 2025).

Although academic disciplines, to a large extent, tend to operate in isolation from one another, drawing on discipline specific concepts, language and ways of thinking, this is not to say that there is no conversation between disciplines. Substantive tax law, for example, draws heavily on economic concepts like profit, so income tax law scholars inherently reflect on economic concepts and categories.[3] Multidisciplinary encounters are common; indeed there is some evidence of fruitful cross-fertilisation of approaches. However, the strictures of academic disciplines, including publication expectations and career progression, undoubtedly constrain the potential for rich and reflexive scholarship, and we find some cases of unhealthy borrowing of concepts and approaches. The emergence of multidisciplinary scholarship makes it even harder for lay travellers to find their way. Common threads bring an element of coherence to relationships between disciples, but the different ways of thinking and doing research remain.

How then can travellers passing through the tax landscape find their way? Those that research tax as academics not only have to grapple with the landscape partitioned by disciplinary boundaries, but also methods for gaining new knowledge that cut across the landscape.

New scholars will generally be based in one of the disciplinary spaces, but in learning their craft, they will find themselves discovering tax research from other parts of the landscape. They will usually be embedded in a single discipline and have obligations to pay due deference to the

[3] We are grateful to Hans Gribnau for this observation.

prevailing norms of that discipline which will be more or less accommodating of interdisciplinary travels depending on the discipline concerned. Old hands sometimes also seek to expand their horizons and explore the landscape to extend their understanding beyond their disciplinary home (Alm, 2012; Oats, 2012)—as this book attempts to do. Some disciplines are more flexible, allowing scholars freedom to borrow from other disciplines, importing ideas and new ways of thinking; others not so much. Economics seems to be particularly unforgiving when scholars stray beyond the mainstream, with some exceptions including the embrace of psychology in behavioural economics, and drawing on legal insights in the law and economics movement.

Those concerned with the practical application of existing tax rules such as practitioners and the commentariat may largely steer clear of the mountains and the wilderness and stay close to the relative safety of urban areas. They certainly avoid the dragons. Those interested in changing the way we tax, for example, finding new things to tax (e.g. cryptocurrency), or new things not to tax (e.g. green technologies) or improving enforcement techniques, may look more closely at the economic vegetation, but are not always able to distinguish weeds from valuable crops. There is now an abundance of studies in academic journals on tax compliance, for example, but not all academic journals are equal, peer review is not always a reliable indicator of quality, nor is the quality of the underpinning assumptions always robust and the waters are increasingly muddied with the advent of artificial intelligence tools such as ChatGPT.

Taxpayers, of course, engage much less with tax scholarship, if at all, but rather they are influenced by how scholarship is absorbed into practical application by policymakers and practitioners; they are one step removed and will therefore find the tax landscape particularly daunting, often get lost or must rely on advisers, professional or otherwise. Many laymen and taxpayers who comply might be quite unaware of tax. They follow the road signs, but most often walk the streets and paths they have always pursued. Others, such as self-employed, might find many obstacles when finding their way through a landscape with many signs, some pointing in opposite directions. Life events—selling a property, inheritance, divorces—may all of a sudden make them aware of new signs and paths. All taxpayers sometimes look into the distance and estimate how far it is to another place; how much of a certain tax that has been or will be paid. An income tax is easy here, but many other taxes are true perception games. A common map might show the actual distance for income tax, although thinking with the topography of the actual landscape to understand how tax affects us is bewildering. It is easy to get lost.

Traps for the Unwary Traveller

Our knowledge of tax—whether it is its laws, payments, impact or the entire system—is in constant flux, as the landscape continuously changes: freak weather conditions change the contours and require new approaches to tax; earthquakes shatter existing ways of thinking. But whatever the shape of the tax landscape, i.e. what we are asked to pay, another form of tax knowledge concerns the actual payment of taxes. How can we know why people pay taxes, or don't as the case may be? With travellers in mind, we identify several 'traps' that await them, causing confusion and potentially misunderstanding. We do not deny the value and importance of the work within these 'traps', but are concerned about uncritical acceptance of their findings.

Persuasive Positivism and the Quest for Quantification

Much of the academic scholarship dealing with tax policy and taxpayer compliance and willingness to pay takes a positivistic approach. This is a specific research approach that is dominant across the social sciences, seeking to find causal relationships, valuing (insisting upon) generalisability and prioritising quantification. Positivism is pleasing because it supposedly provides objective and concrete answers. Politicians, influencers and other decision-makers love it.

The vast majority of positivistic research uses quantitative methods, which obscure many underlying assumptions from the view of those without mathematical prowess. Numbers 'have come to be endowed with a form of truth that has the authority to guide or govern us' (Kurunmäki et al., 2016). Quantification transforms quality into quantity, subjective experience into objective knowledge. 'Once numbers are created … they become enrolled and translated by different users and built into institutions in ways that may make them difficult to change or abandon' (Mennicken & Espeland, 2019). There is usually social and cognitive distance between the creators of datasets and those who use them. Users, who produce conclusions based on the datasets, often take data as given and have little interest in how the numbers were collected, coded and cleaned (Desrosieres, 2001). Steffen Mau (2019) describes quantification as a cult, driven in part by the popularity of concepts such as transparency and evidence basing, where quantified rankings and evaluation are prominent, many in the service of some form of neoliberalism.

Annoyingly, much research in this tradition does not present itself overtly as positivistic, especially when it is firmly entrenched as the only valid form of inquiry. Economics, political science and psychology are academic disciplines that lead the quest for quantifying ways of trying to understand tax compliance. Academics write primarily for those within their own disciplines where they share a common language, assumptions and ways of thinking. There is often little need to explain these things; they are readily understood by peers. But because positivism is often unstated and unexplained, there are traps for the unwary in taking the results of such studies into policymaking and practice.

Enticing Economics

Economics certainly permeates most ways of thinking about tax and underpins many ideas about it including those embraced by policymakers and the wider populace. Importantly, the field of economics extends beyond the ivory tower of academia and we find economists revered in government policymaking as well as supranational bodies such as the International Monetary Fund (IMF) and World Bank, NGOs such as think tanks and consultancy firms, cementing its position of dominance. This dominance is both the discipline of economics and the holders of economic qualifications and expertise as economic professionals (e.g. Fourcade et al., 2015).

Economics remains largely impervious to critique, Japanese knotweed rather than fields of wheat. Robert Skidelsky (2020), for example, is scathing in his criticism: 'by assuming a certain type of human being ... [economics] underestimates the cost of its promises ... [and] its path to re-engineering human behaviour is littered with broken societies' (p. 191).

The economic perspective on tax is often concerned with how a certain tax will influence other parts of the landscape. Anything is framed; mostly about other economic issues but its way of thinking has also been used extensively to model other societal issues: for example, Michael G. Allingham and Agnar Sandmo's (1972) seminal model of tax evasion that has been endlessly cited, modified and updated. A very simplified conclusion of Allingham and Sandmo's article is that taxpayers always try to maximise their income in relation to tax payment and penalty fees.

Accordingly, a taxpayer will report and pay just enough tax, weighing the outcome of successful tax evasion against being caught and paying penalties. Regardless of where in the landscape the taxpayer is, the starting point is always the same; it is about *measuring* the relations or *assessing* output between different places in the topography. Although both assumptions and results may be surrounded by caveats, these are often lost in the weeds of persuasive numbers.

Economics as an academic discipline has long held, certainly since the early twentieth century, a hegemonic position in tax scholarship (Benshalom, 2021b). Economic models seek to predict how taxation makes an impact on economies. But in so doing, these models also shape the way taxation is understood. For example, when we agree on a discourse that taxation is good for society, we navigate towards a more generous tax policy and so do the models. On the other hand, when taxation is seen as being bad for society, as in neoliberal thinking, it is seen as being an unnecessary cost and the economic models follow suit. Economics has given us optimal tax theory, and who can argue against anything that is supposed to be optimal. But optimal tax theory has a dark side and has been criticised for the assumptions it makes (e.g. Sugin, 2010; Shaviro, 2016). Ilan Benshalom (2021a) questions why so much of the optimal tax theory research 'has not transcended the theoretical literature to become viable tax policy prescriptions' (p. 197).

It is important to note that apart from developing elaborate and convincing models, much economic scholarship, including optimal tax theory, is also founded on assumptions that tend to go unquestioned. Although economics has largely moved away from *Homo economicus*, assumptions of bounded rationality and utility maximisation remain (Bearer-Friend et al., 2022). In the metaphor of topography, there is more to describing the landscape than just relating different places to each other. The field of economics has a remarkable lack of self-awareness of the naturalisation of concepts and ideas within its work (Scott, 2023). The absorption of neoliberalism and its transformation from rhetoric to dogma is one example, as can be seen in economics textbooks (as analysed by Zuidhof, 2014). Scott argues that neoliberalism has become invisible to orthodox economics. Over many years it has become increasingly insular, in part due to the narrow training received by economists, who very rarely now study the history of economic thought as they once did.

In recent years we have seen other disciplines taking an economic perspective and using economic conceptualisations, absorbing them subtly or more overtly into joint ventures. This could also be viewed as the colonisation of other fields by economic thinking. We find this in law, with the emergence of law and economics as a sub-discipline, but also in economic psychology, economic sociology and political economy.

As we live in 'an era of measurability' (Bornemark, 2018), results from economic research are indeed enticing.

Inviting Individualism and Beguiling Behaviouralism

In many of our disciplinary spaces, the focus of research is the mind: behaviour and attitudes of individuals as individuals. Methodological individualism is inviting because it allows researchers to constrain their field of vision, and thereby ignore, or at least downplay, the complexities of social and cultural influences. In this approach, it is assumed that social practice is the aggregation of individual practices.

The rise of experimentation as a method in psychology, economics and political science has led to a veritable jungle of findings about taxpayer compliance behaviour. Behavioural economics aims to take control of the research environment and rigour of method to extremes, such that the research question at hand often gets lost amid concerns about experimental design, research participants must be monetarily incentivised with the price of a few pints of beer or else they will not tell the truth in the laboratory. The pursuit of rigour overshadows dubious assumptions about cause and effect. Regardless of what the landscape actually looks like—soil, climate, quality of the forestry—the experimental toolbox makes sure that the map will always be right. With experiments, they may also attempt to understand why the map does not illustrate the actual landscape. Results from experiments can make slow changes to the map. More problematic is that old findings based on erroneous assumptions risk steering our contemporary understanding of changed landscapes.

The behavioural turn across the social sciences has privileged methodological individualism under which it is assumed that the aggregation of individual behaviour can say something about societal values. People are said to be brought into the picture, but those are very simple people. They are more like robots who only have very limited choices for action. Examples are surveys used to find out about perceptions and attitudes towards paying taxes. Measuring soft concepts is problematic but portrayed as simple using assumptions and proxies. Likert scales, yes and no questions, gradings, etc. are used to depict the complicated world of tax.

Aggregating incommensurable soft concepts, for example, measuring tax morale is also problematic, but the downsides of doing so are glossed over as models and methods become entrenched ways of doing tax research, not seeing the forest for the trees. Often these are followed unreflexively by acolytes bound by the constraints imposed by the disciplinary mainstream that dictate who succeeds and who fails. As James Alm and Mattias Kasper (2022, p. 10) confidently assert, 'It is difficult for standard expected utility models to explain … responses to audits, and it is only with behavioural economics considerations that these results can be explained'. Behavioural economics seems to be, at least to explain tax compliance, the only game in town.

Captivating Categorisations

Knowledge about why people pay tax largely comes from research that categorises people in various ways: gender, geographic location, class, citizenship status, ethnicity, religion, etc. Although categorising is a fundamental human behaviour to survive in the world, we see considerable peril in heavy reliance on this in developing tax knowledge, especially knowledge of tax compliance. Although classifying people into groups aids in the organisation and simplification of helping people to be compliant with tax rules, social categorisation of people qua taxpayers also has several perils. These general conclusions about people are important to recall, especially when we deal with such a complex practice as taxation.

First, categorisation of taxpayers can lead to *stereotyping*. The ascription of individuals' characteristics is often oversimplified and thus inaccurate. It may also become fixed and stick with a group for the foreseeable future. This can result in unfair assumptions about individuals based on their group membership rather than other attributes or actions. Second, the act of categorisation may lead to *prejudice*. Categorising individuals into groups can foster prejudice, or prejudgement, leading to irrational, negative attitudes towards members of certain groups. This can manifest in various ways, including racism, sexism, ageism and other forms of discrimination. A classic example from tax research is that the self-employed have a larger propensity to not pay the correct tax. There is certainly both avoidance and evasion of taxes among this group; however, there might also be lack of knowledge or simply that third-party tax reporting tends to be more accurate (Bobek et al., 2007). A third peril with categorisation is *discrimination*. Prejudice stemming from social categorisation can escalate into discrimination, where individuals or groups are treated unfairly or unjustly because of their membership in a particular social category. This can affect opportunities, resources and rights, leading to systemic inequalities. Fourth is in-group *bias* and out-group *homogeneity*. Social categorisation often reinforces in-group bias, where individuals show preference for members of their own group (in-group) over those of other groups (out-group). An additional negative result is that people tend to perceive out-group members as more similar to each other than they really are (out-group homogeneity effect), which may further entrench stereotyping. In societal discourse there is a prevalent view that immigrants receive more social welfare benefits as they are less likely to be employed (Örstadius, 2024). For tax research, this might also be detrimental for societal tax compliance as non-members of identified social categories might be influenced: 'If they do not pay their fair share of tax, why should I?' Fifth is *social identity* threat. Simply knowing that belonging to a group that is negatively stereotyped in society can lead to social identity threats. This means that individuals fear being judged or treated according to stereotypes, potentially impacting performance, self-esteem and the willingness to engage in certain activities or contexts. Overemphasis on social categories can overshadow individual identity, leading people to be seen primarily as representatives of a group rather than as individuals. In tax research, this can lead to adopting certain tax behaviour perceiving other members of 'my category' to do so.

Importantly, many tax authorities use categorisations to inform their tax collection strategies. Pioneering work by the Australian Centre for Tax System Integrity in the 1990s, for example, led to the embrace of the compliance pyramid in which taxpayers are categorised according to their behaviour, and enforcement strategies devised for each category. This way of thinking about tax collection has spread to many other countries, including the UK. Similar forms of categorisation can be seen in tax gap calculations. In the UK, for example, attempts are made to measure the tax gap by reference to type of taxpayer behaviour, for example, distinguishing taxpayer error, avoidance and criminal attacks. Yet, there are disastrous examples such as the Dutch *Toeslagenaffaire*[4] (Hadwick & Lan, 2021) and the Australian *Robodebt*

[4]The Dutch *Toeslagenaffaire* (childcare benefits scandal) meant that parents were sometimes wrongly accused of making fraudulent benefit claims, resulting in demands to repay their allowances in full. The simple categorisation made by algorithms affected especially parents with foreign backgrounds.

scandal[5] (van Rooy, 2025), both having devastating effects for the wrongly automatically selected taxpayers. Yet other tax administrations recognise the perils of one-sighted pursuit strategies of certain taxpayer categories. The former chief strategist at the Swedish Tax Agency compared speeding with making tax errors: 'we know young men with fast cars have a tendency to speed, yet we are not only after speeding young men—we want to catch all who speed'.

While social categorisation is an inherent part of human cognition, awareness of its potential downsides can help mitigate its negative impacts. Efforts to foster cross-group understanding, challenge stereotypes and promote inclusive environments are essential in addressing the perils of social categorisation.

Our Research Approach

We consider ourselves to be interpretive and critical scholars, willing to challenge mainstream ways of thinking and calling for more depth and reflection, unpacking the epistemological and ontological assumptions of tax knowledge, dancing with dragons.

Arguably, all research involves acts of interpretation. Interpretation is fundamental to legal scholars; for example, it is the very essence of researching and also practising law. Yet, interpretivism has a special meaning in social science research and is often contrasted with positivism. Where a positivist approach entails developing hypotheses for testing, an interpretivist develops research questions from issues that seem puzzling, maybe even based on personal experience, and seeks to understand them using insights from people. An interpretivist believes that reality is socially constructed, subjective, and multiple, rather than objective and measurable. The focus is on inductively understanding the *why* behind human behavior by interpreting the meanings, emotions, and values people assign to their experiences—in this case of paying tax. Where positivists look at supposedly objective data for generalisable causal mechanisms using constrained techniques, an interpretivist approach is iterative. Research questions may therefore alter and new puzzles arise as the research progresses.

Critical approaches are rare in the tax landscape. We see the critical scholar aiming to depict the landscape for what it is, questioning the map, the signposts, the yields, the morale. For readers interested in pursuing a

[5] The *Robodebt* scheme was an unlawful method of automated debt assessment and recovery implemented in Australia 2016. The scheme was an automated replacement of the formerly manual system of calculating overpayments and issuing debt notices to welfare recipients. It was criticised by media, academics, advocacy groups and politicians due to allegations of false or incorrectly calculated debt notices being issued.

critical path, Oats et al. (2025) suggest some 'critical moves'—pathways for critique that can be taken to move beyond the mainstream within each discipline.

> [T]here are many different forms of scholarship that can be thought of as being critical. Some scholars are 'critical of'; identifying fissures and flaws in practices, understandings and recommendations, often with radical, disruptive intent. Others are 'critical with', drawing on insights from social theory or other disciplinary perspectives to probe, question and reinterpret received views. (Oats et al., 2025, p. 8)

Our approach to researching tax is different to that of scholars who adopt positivist and quantitative approaches. We share a concern about the stultifying effects of quantification and seek to bring to the fore qualitative approaches that take taxpayers seriously, trying to recognise their intentions, their aims and actual practices. In addition, we try to break free from disciplinary strictures, travelling across the whole of the tax landscape and not confining ourselves to the constraints of any single academic discipline.

Our research aim is to take people seriously in all their complexity. This might sound a bit exaggerated, even preposterous, but our aim is to apply methods trying to understand participants' views and practices on tax to the fullest extent possible. To cite an influential tax researcher from the economic discipline, we aim to contribute to the '"full house" of strategies to measure, explain, and control the "full house" of behaviors and motivations' (Alm, 2012, p. 65). This is why we apply ethnographic methods.

The ethnographer is a wanderer and risks going astray in the wilderness looking for the unseen, the hidden and the forgotten parts of the landscape. Applying an ethnographic perspective means aiming to understand the context within which people operate. It provides rich and detailed material in interlocutors' own words, which includes engaging with their feelings and emotions. An ethnographic perspective may also uncover hidden insights, stalagmites in an underground cavern. Ethnographic methods allow people to formulate their views, opinions and concerns in their own words. We believe this to be an important addition to existing research that mostly builds on previous research, using hypotheses formulated by the researchers themselves. Applying an ethnographic perspective and methods provides a comprehensive, nuanced and empathetic understanding of human behaviours, practices and experiences.

By engaging participants in both individual, semi-structured interviews and roundtable discussions with others, we acquired new insights. Among them was the very topic of this book. As we show in Chap. 2, talking about belonging had more meaning for participants in relation to tax than exploring the issue of citizenship.

Reflections

Thinking with topography in describing the landscape of scholarly research in taxation allows us to take one approach to the complicated landscape of taxation. We have consciously been provocative in our descriptions of the various academic disciplines and their methods. Although some may disagree, there is more than a grain of truth in our assessment—there might even be bushels. Political arguments about tax often have their starting point in research reports and economic assessments. To separate the wheat from the chaff, the premises and methodologies applied have to be thoroughly scrutinised. Taxation is just too important a subject for the economy *and* for society; it needs to be handled with care and responsibility.

A critical perspective on tax does not offer *the* solution, far from it. But such research opens up perspectives often previously unseen and may provide fertile insights when society changes. This is what we will lay out in the following chapters where we describe how a critical perspective on tax takes shape when we engage with taxpayers often previously overlooked.

References

Allingham, M. G., and A. Sandmo. 1972. Income tax evasion: A theoretical analysis. *Journal of Public Economics* 1:323–338.

Alm, J. 2012. Measuring, explaining, and controlling tax evasion: Lessons from theory, experiments, and field studies. *International Tax and Public Finance* 19 (1): 54–77.

Alm, J., and M. Kasper. 2022. Using behavioural economics to understand tax compliance. *Economic and Political Studies.* https://doi.org/10.1080/20954816.2022.2117676.

Bearer-Friend, J., A. Glogower, A. J. Kleiman, and C. G. Wallace. 2022. Taxation and law and political economy. *Ohio State Law Journal* 83 (3): 471–528.

Benshalom, I. 2021a. The rise of inequality and the fall of tax equity: A call for a non-ideal distributive tax theory. *British Tax Review* 2:195–220.

Benshalom, I. 2021b. Recalibrating moral feasibility boundaries of taxation. *Tax Law Review* 74 (2): 211–258.

Björklund Larsen, L., and H. J. Lauth. 2025. Fiscal citizenship from an interdisciplinary perspective: Opportunities and risks of researching across disciplines. *World Tax Journal* 17 (3): https://doi.org/10.59403/2pd1p6j.

Bobek, D. D., R. W. Roberts, and J. T. Sweeney. 2007. The social norms of tax compliance: Evidence from Australia, Singapore, and the United States. *Journal of Business Ethics* 74:49–64.

Bornemark, J. 2018. *Det omätbaras renässans: En uppgörelse med pedanternas världsherravälde*. 1st ed. Volante.

van Brederode, R. F. 2022. Introduction: The value of a political theory for the proper application of taxation. In *Political philosophy and taxation: A history from the enlightenment to the present*, 1–50. Springer Nature Singapore.

Brinkmann, S., M. Jacobsen, and S. Kristiansen. 2020. Historical overview of qualitative research in the social sciences. In *The Oxford handbook of qualitative research*, ed. P. Leavy, 2nd ed., 24–58. Oxford Library of Psychology.

Clemens, E. 1999. Review: Good reasons to stop avoiding taxes. *Law and Social Inquiry* 24 (2): 517–531.

Desrosieres, A. 2001. How 'real' are statistics? Four possible attitudes. *Social Research* 68:339–355.

Fourcade, M., E. Ollion, and Y. Algan. 2015. The superiority of economists. *Journal of Economic Perspectives* 29 (1): 89–114. https://doi.org/10.1257/jep.29.1.89.

Hadwick, D., and S. Lan. 2021. Lessons to be learned from the Dutch childcare allowance scandal. *World Tax Journal* 13 (4): 609–645.

Kurunmäki, L., A. Mennicken, and P. Miller. 2016. Quantifying, economising and marketising: Democratising the social sphere? *Sociologie du Travail* 58 (4): 390–402. https://doi.org/10.1016/j.soctra.2016.09.018.

Mau, S. 2019. *The metric society: On the quantification of the social*. Polity Press.

Mennicken, A., and W. N. Espeland. 2019. What's new with numbers? Sociological approaches to the study of quantification. *Annual Review of Sociology* 45:223–245.

Oats, L. 2012. Tax as a social and institutional practice. In *Taxation: A fieldwork research handbook*, ed. L. Oats, 3–8. Routledge.

Oats, L., C. Edgley, and E. Mulligan. 2025. Critical perspectives on taxation: In praise of heterophony. *Critical Perspectives on Accounting* 101:102794.

Örstadius, K. 2024, March 18. *Fakta i frågan: Är utrikesfödda bidragsberoende?* Dagens Nyheter.

Pascale, C.-M. 2011. *Cartographies of knowledge: Exploring qualitative epistemologies*. Sage.

van Rooy, D. 2025. A cognitive science framework could prevent harmful public policy decisions involving AI. *Behavioral Science & Policy* 11 (1): 33–43. https://doi.org/10.1177/23794607251336099.

Scott, T. 2023. Bourdieu, Lacan and field theory: Neoliberal doxa in the economic field. *Theory Culture and Society* 41 (2): 113–130. https://doi.org/10.1177/02632764231178646.

Shaviro, D. 2016. The mapmaker's dilemma in evaluating high-end inequality. *University of Miami Law Review* 71 (1): 83–159.

Skidelsky, R. 2020. *What's wrong with economics? A primer for the perplexed*. Yale University Press.

Sugin, L. 2010. A philosophical objection to the optimal tax model. *Tax Law Review* 64:229–281.

Zuidhof, P. 2014. Thinking like an economist: The neoliberal politics of the economics textbook. *Review of Social Economy* 72 (2): 157–185. https://doi.org/10.1080/00346764.2013.872952.

CHAPTER 2

From Citizenship to Belonging

Abstract When speaking to participants in our UK fieldwork in 2021–2022, citizenship was important but mainly thought of in terms of a formal, legal phenomenon. When talking about tax, participants seemed more comfortable speaking of belonging. An abductive approach was used to make sense of what the participants told us. Fiscal citizenship, which is where this project started, is used by scholars to capture rights and obligations associated with payment of taxes, often by reference to the social contract. Belonging, however, appears to us to be a richer concept with which to explore fiscal relations, in this case for middle-class professional immigrants to the UK.

Keywords Fiscal citizenship • Fiscal belonging • Social contract • Tax compliance • Ethnography • Abductive analysis

As we explained in Chap. 1, we are critical, interpretive researchers seeking to delve deeply into the issues we find intriguing. This includes research that does not seem to agree with what is observed in the world around us, or contradictions between what people do and say in the tax arena. We are driven by curiosity which means that we constantly question what we find. We are not looking to find causal relationships or definitive truths, rather we want to probe received understandings and better comprehend the phenomena we observe. It is in this spirit that we approached the question

L. Björklund Larsen, L. Oats, *Crossing Borders, Sharing Burdens*,
https://doi.org/10.1007/978-3-031-99394-7_2

of migrants' willingness to pay tax, in particular in relation to the concept of fiscal citizenship. Our fieldwork, took us on a journey from thinking in terms of citizenship, to thinking in terms of belonging.

In this chapter we first describe our methodology, how we approached and conducted our study. We then reflect on where the insights of our participants take us, first by discussing the concept of citizenship, by looking at how this relates to matters fiscal in the guise of fiscal citizenship and finally by arriving at belonging, as a broader but arguably thicker concept than citizenship to describe a form of attachment.

Methodology: Fields, Fieldwork and Analysis

A field is where our research question takes us. A field may be geographically bounded. It may focus on a specific group of people sharing ethnicity, religion, political views or just having something in common (Hannerz, 2001). It may be an organisation such as work, voluntary engagement or a sphere of practical activity. Yet, a field is not necessarily constrained to one location; it can be multi-sited (Marcus, 1995), following people and their actions—always in pursuit of addressing the research questions.

This also means that any field is contextual. It is crucial to be cognisant of the prevailing social, economic, cultural and political background and conditions when the data was collected. In this we differ from those scholars who adopt a more universalistic stance that sees individual attitudes and behaviour as existing outside of time and space.

Our field is both geographically bounded, in the sense that our participants were or had been residents of the UK, and focused on a specific group of people sharing a common experience—that of being a migrant and interacting with the UK tax system.

The field is thus where, when and among whom we conduct our fieldwork; the collection of data. It takes place outside the confines of a laboratory, library or workplace setting. Fieldwork can use a variety of methods of collecting data but engages with people in all their complexity. Examples of fieldwork studies in tax include tax policy development (Rogers & Oats, 2022), legislative changes (Ormeno-Pèrez & Oats, 2023), tax compliance (Wynter & Oats, 2018), tax audits (Boll, 2014), the internal workings of a revered tax administration (Björklund Larsen, 2017), the tax profession (Killian et al., 2023; Mulligan & Oats, 2016) or how democratisation is linked to revenue collection (Guyer, 1992). Fieldwork studies always engage 'with what actually happens in the real world when tax rules and regulations are put into play' (Oats, 2012, p. 5).

We were interested in migrants' willingness to pay tax and wanted to hear their concerns. Our fieldwork thus engaged in discussions with people, mainly migrants, who were, or had been, residents of the UK, with or without citizenship. The first question was what to ask about; what were the issues around taxation that concerned migrants? We decided on a two-step fieldwork: first exploratory roundtables allowing people to discuss issues that seemed important to them. The insights from the roundtables would then be used to conduct individual ethnographic and in-depth interviews.

The Fiscal Citizenship project started during the global pandemic, in March 2021. In June 2021, we started our fieldwork with two virtual roundtable events with four and five participants, respectively. Our aim was to discuss issues around tax and citizenship and we invited middle-class migrant professionals with knowledge of the tax system. There were three reasons for our choice of participants.

First, taxes can be seen as a sensitive and intimate issue and not something people at large are comfortable discussing. Second, we felt that knowledgeable participants would be able to alert us to issues and concerns that would be worthy of further investigation by way of semi-structured ethnographic interviews. Third, we were conscious of how intimidating a virtual environment can be for novices; the people we chose for our roundtables were all comfortable with using digital communication software in their work environment. Consent was given in advance to record these sessions, which lasted around 90 minutes in both cases.

The invitation was very straightforward. It included a description of the Fiscal Citizenship project and described the digital roundtables as an 'exploratory event to share ideas about attitudes towards taxes and tax morale, in particular when moving from one country to another'. In particular we stated that we were interested in 'issues that cause concern when starting life in a new country in relation to reporting and paying taxes'. The roundtable discussions circled around the following topics: a description of themselves and why they moved to the UK; which country they call home and how they describe its tax culture; where they think attitudes about tax originates; what it means to be a citizen and how citizenship relates to tax; the most urgent issue to address regarding migrants and tax; and finally if there were other issues to address that we had omitted.

Participants were very generous in sharing personal experiences and suggestions for our research. The outcome of the roundtables provided us with some important insights into aspects of the migrant experience that informed our interview schedule.

Tax may be a very technical subject and people's understanding of tax rules and systems often diverge from the facts. As a traveller qua interviewer in the wild, it is therefore vital that the questions make interviewees reflect on *their views* and their *understanding* of tax. In the interviews, we discussed aspects of citizenship, their practical engagement with tax authorities and finally their views and attitudes on tax. We delved into various aspects of what it means to be a citizen including how they see the rights and obligations associated with citizenship respectively. We never used the term 'fiscal citizenship' explicitly. Instead we focused on the one hand on being a member of society, community and nation (citizenship broadly speaking) and on the other hand what taxation (the fiscal component) means. Following the outcome of the roundtables, one issue of special interest was how our participants spoke about home and belonging rather than citizenship.

Belonging thus became an issue we dealt with more deeply in the subsequent semi-structured interviews we conducted with a range of people who had moved to the UK. Their participation was secured in the first instance through personal contacts and then through snowballing. More than 20 in-depth interviews were conducted in the second half of 2021 and during spring 2022. When possible we met face to face in meetings lasting one hour on average. Participants came from all continents, had worked and lived in the UK for quite some time, and had importantly been paying tax in the country. Tax is a sensitive subject and to ensure that they felt free to express their views and in order to protect participants' identity, their names have been altered and their native country is referenced as a region. As with the roundtable participants, interviewees were generous with sharing their perceptions and experiences.

Ours is an abductive approach. Abductive conclusions do not eliminate uncertainty or doubt, rather our analysis is based on 'best available' or 'most likely'. While inductive reasoning draws general conclusions that apply to many situations, abductive conclusions are confined to the particular observations in question. However, abductive analysis takes into account the knowledge of tax we have amassed over the years, including our position in the tax research topography. Reading and analysing our interviews, we interpret and get a feeling for how views on taxation are articulated. As critical social scientists, we can read the signs and follow the roads and paths outlined. We can climb the ridges to get an overview of the scenery and dig in the historical sediments. But we can also venture out in the wilderness and criss-cross the streets aiming to understand what people actually think and do. It is the most accurate analysis we can offer based on our position in the landscape.

We found three interrelated areas on which our study shone new light: belonging, culture and reciprocity. But our starting point was citizenship.

There are certainly many who relate paying tax to citizenship, but citizenship is often spoken about in very pragmatic terms—of having a passport, of being able to vote and having working rights, etc. Furthermore, asking about citizenship made many participants search for a correct answer. Citizenship became a very etic term, meaning that they tried to remember the definition of citizenship as something they had read and learnt about once upon a time, but also thinking hard about the rights and obligations it entails.

We need to note that these are people's opinions on tax and about belonging. It would be simplistic to say that our participants willingly pay tax. Although most recognise the importance of taxes and the need for paying them, well, it is a necessary evil. What they expressed in common was a quite unified view that people with little income, the 'poor', and the 'filthy' rich are those who are most likely to avoid and evade paying tax but for different reasons. It is the well-informed middle class that to a large extent pay taxes due. As Anne, a young woman from Northern Europe, said, 'the crowd in the middle, maybe they are carrying a lot of the brunt of that responsibility' of paying tax. One should reflexively ask if this mirrors our participants who seldom, if ever, admitted to not having paid tax (although they regarded some as not legitimate).

One question for us is how the sense of belonging relates to people's views on taxation. We find it astonishing that tax is hardly mentioned in much of the writing on belonging; if mentioned it is *en passant*. This seems strange, particularly in jurisdictions where public services are to a large extent funded by taxes. Perhaps this is due to a narrow definition of tax as an economic transaction, not taking into account its social consequences and impact.

Alongside belonging, our participants also raised questions for us about the notion of tax culture. Coming from very different backgrounds, many of our interviewees rather talked about the fiscal cultures in their home countries and their view of the British fiscal culture. Fiscal culture here is broader than tax culture and includes government spending as welfare. Finally, despite the separation of academic scholarship on tax and welfare, we found our interviewees insisting on bringing the two together in the notion of reciprocity.

The wider project that this work comes from is called fiscal citizenship. How did we get from fiscal citizenship to fiscal belonging? The starting point is citizenship, because we are interested in migrants for whom citizenship is more important than for a native.

Citizenship is a contested concept that is interpreted differently by scholars with different visions of how society works. Citizenship, however defined, is particularly important to some migrants, as a symbol of acceptance into a new society. If we think of citizenship as culturally produced, and manifesting in both formal and informal ways, we can then think of citizenship as a form of capital. Citizenship in this view can be a strategic concept. It can also be a mechanism of distinction, rendering migrants without citizenship as 'other' (Bauder, 2008; Vicol, 2023). From citizenship, our first move is to fiscal citizenship, which is the part of citizenship that encompasses transfers, usually monetary, from citizens to state and from state to citizens. Modern citizenship comprises rights on the one hand and obligations on the other. In one view, citizenship defines belonging, through entitlements flowing from service and payment of taxes, the monetary and non-monetary contributions such as work or parenting that secure specified and unspecified rights (Isin & Turner, 2007). A considerable amount of scholarship, however, focuses mainly on rights and largely neglects questions of obligation or duty.

The right to citizenship is different from the rights flowing from being certified as a citizen (Tjernberg, 2010). Certified citizenship confers a legal status, but importantly citizenship also confers a social status. Material trappings of citizenship such as a passport or identity card confirm citizenship status. However, citizenship as a social practice may extend beyond a legal status within a geographical space, particularly in an age of borders weakened by new technologies such as telecommunications and transport (Isin & Turner, 2007). Citizenship can thus also be understood as a cultural practice when people perform, negotiate and experience it in daily life (Marshall, 1950), even across borders in transnational settings (Ong, 1999).

Certainly, there are many images and ways of thinking of citizenship. Contractarians take a more individualistic view based around a metaphorical contract between individuals and the state such that a reciprocal relationship ensues; individual freedom is surrendered in order to secure state protection (Dean, 2004). Solidarists take a collectivist view built around cooperation and shared sovereignty.

Migration involves myriad motivations and throws up many questions. What features should be used to determine the distinction between visitor and citizen—length of stay, reason for immigration, strength of attachment?

Recognising the complexities of citizenship as a concept throws doubt on how we can understand fiscal citizenship.

Fiscal Citizenship

Fiscal citizenship is an aspect of citizenship that has been largely overlooked, as noted by Fred Twine (1994), with some notable exceptions. There is much to be learnt from the scholarship around fiscal citizenship, which scholars engaging with the idea approach in different ways.

There are differing views about what the 'fiscal' in fiscal citizenship means. Is it only taxes? Does it include other forms of financial contribution? Does the contribution have to be financial?

James Sparrow, for example, includes more broadly investments in public funding, such as Americans' purchase of wartime bonds during World War II (WWII) (Sparrow, 2008). In his view, in addition to the extension of income tax to those on lower incomes, public ownership of savings bonds served to 'bolster the postwar fiscal regime and democratize the meaning of fiscal citizenship' (2008, p. 264). This is close to Ajay Mehrotra's description of Americans' relation to the state articulated through growing democratic institutions and policies during the twentieth century. Although his analysis is narrowed to taxes, the increased fiscal revenue makes possible individual economic opportunities and wealth redistribution for the population (2015). Fiscal citizenship is thus closely intertwined with how the state can engage in and also boost the market economy for the benefit of the larger population.

While recognising that some scholars take an expansive view of what 'fiscal' is, we are primarily interested in taxation and ask what are the different ways in which the concept of fiscal citizenship has been mobilised by tax scholars. Without claiming to be comprehensive we identify three forms which the concept of fiscal citizenship has taken across the disciplinary landscape: as political engagement, as a social contract and as tax compliance.[1] The first two of these more explicitly engage with the concept of fiscal citizenship. The last can be seen as a very specific form of fiscal citizenship, although scholarship on tax compliance does not usually reference the concept directly. All three are interrelated and may overlap depending on authors' viewpoint and ideological position.

[1] We are indebted to our fiscal citizenship project colleagues in this overview. As a group, in the early days of the project, we spent considerable time discussing, virtually being unable to meet face to face, the nature of fiscal citizenship and how it has been approached in prior scholarship.

Fiscal Citizenship as Political Engagement

Some scholars see fiscal citizenship as political engagement, as a direct negotiation tool between state and citizen. It has been used to argue for claims against the state (Freund, 2019), for example, demands for political representation linked to the payment of taxes. Fiscal citizenship as political engagement can also be seen in citizens withholding tax payments in protest against the approach of a particular political administration (ibid.). Fiscal citizenship can further be used to fend off a strong fiscal state.[2] In defence of retaining personal income tax in the USA rather than replacing it with a value added tax, Richard Musgrave observed that without personal income tax 'the essential linkage between citizenship and fiscal responsibility is broken' (1997, p. 157).

Assaf Likhovski believes that 'taxation is not only a revenue raising tool ... but also a method for social construction—a way to create a shared identity and common notions of citizenship and community' (2017, p. 14). In the historical study of Israeli taxation, fiscal citizenship appears as a civic duty but also as a political tool to increase citizen engagement (2017). This comes close to Sandra Morgen and Jennifer Erickson's attempt to 'define and analyse fiscal citizenship as the discourses and meanings attributable to tax paying as a particular relationship to the state, society and community' (2017, p. 55). Along the same lines but emphasising that it is constantly subject to change, fiscal citizenship is described by Emanuela Guano in a study of contemporary Italy. Here fiscal citizenship is the 'seemingly capricious application of rights, duties and entitlements' among people defined as different categories (2010, p. 487). Fiscal citizenship is constantly negotiated along and across the split between equity and denial of the same, constantly mediated by the state.

Perhaps not as distinctly a political tool, Isaac Martin and co-authors note that taxation is a crucial element in state building and creates generalised reciprocity among the population (2010), regardless of the capacity in which we act: consumers, homeowners, wage earners or investors.

Fiscal Citizenship as a Social Contract

The idea of a social contract has a long history and was given a new lease of life during and in the wake of the Covid-19 pandemic (Burnyeat &

[2] We are grateful to Ralf Schenk for this insight.

Sheild Johansson, 2022, p. 222). It is a view of the relationship between state and society from the top of the mountain, to invoke our topology, embraced by philosophically minded legal scholars amongst others.

Some scholars articulate fiscal citizenship explicitly as a negotiated social contract between the state and a class of actors whereby rights are exchanged for obligation in the form of tax liabilities. Alex Freund (2019) sees the social contract as giving rise to ethical obligations for both parties, citizen and state. The focus here is on groups of actors, individuals or organisations and the content of rights and obligations that may vary between different classes of actors. The social contract is seen as a bargain, to be renegotiated as context changes, for example, generational shifts. Mehrotra firmly associates fiscal citizenship with a social contract: 'fiscal citizenship institutionalises a social contract between the state and its citizens, between the sovereign and its subjects, formalising our obligations to each other as members of an "imagined community." It also signifies who is a member of such a community, or how wide we draw the circle of "we"' (Mehrotra, 2017, p. 285). He later goes further by stating '[taxation] is, in short, an instantiation of the social contract'.

Charlotte Schmidt and Eva Matthaei develop a model of fiscal citizenship based on the related concepts of a social contract and reciprocity. They conceive of fiscal citizenship as a 'multidimensional trait composed of behaviours, attitudes, and identification of citizens toward the state and their fellow citizens that emerge through taxation'. Their ambitious use of the model allows it to be extended to country level so as to describe the 'overall fiscal and civic climate within society' (Schmidt & Matthaei, 2024, p. 55). The model synthesises tax compliance models and citizenship concepts to develop a concept tree that is then further developed into measurable factors.

Notwithstanding the intuitive appeal of and enthusiasm for a social contract as the basis for fiscal citizenship, we share the concerns of the fiscal anthropologists who question the efficacy of the social contract, which has 'become a pervasive way to think about state-society relations by slipping into common parlance, unmoored from the specificity of its philosophical heritage' (Burnyeat & Sheild Johansson, 2022, p. 224). There are many people across our wonderful globe who regard tax as coercive (Roitman, 2005; Bäumer Escobar, 2020) and prefer to engage in a 'social contract' with their church by paying tithes as some Ghanaians in Accra do (Kauppinen, 2020) or as the inhabitants of Cochabamba, Bolivia, who rather pay taxes as a way of gaining independence from an intruding state

(Shield Johansson, 2020). The idea of tax as a social contract is largely a Western idea, arguably more strongly felt in countries with civil law systems, however adopted by tax authorities worldwide.

Fiscal Citizenship as Tax Compliance

Some scholars take a more narrow view—that fiscal citizenship comprises compliance with tax obligations in terms of paying taxes due at the right time. There is a large body of literature that tries to understand why citizens choose to evade paying taxes and more recently, why they choose to pay taxes that they could otherwise evade. Much of this research is conducted using insights from behavioural science, by public economists, psychologists and at the interface between the two, economic psychology and behavioural economics. The methods of choice are surveys and experiments. While this literature generally does not explicitly reference the concept of fiscal citizenship, it is implicit and several fellow members of fiscal citizenship research took compliance as an aspect of fiscal citizenship worthy of investigation.

Citizenship, especially in American scholarship, is seen as tightly connected to taxation. Non-citizens have been an easy target for exclusionary politics in terms of taxation as they are seen not to pay-up yet benefit from public funding. Tax plays an important role in *both* citizenship and community membership claims, although this has frequently been overlooked as tax scholarship often has a narrower focus, e.g. ability to pay or benefit theories (Davis, 2024). Citizenship is not only a legal category, but also a social imaginary (ibid., p. 170) as people can be *formal* citizens (having acquired legal status) but also *perform* as citizens (behaving both socially and culturally as other citizens) (Davis, 2017). Performing includes tax behaviour. Tax scholarship mostly forgets to pay attention to the broader, colloquial, definitions of citizenship, rather, narrowly focusing on benefits theory in terms of efficiency and 'ability to pay'. For immigrants[3] 'participation in economic life, including payment of taxes, is one of many indicators of their moral claim to citizenship. It's not about benefits and burdens; it's about belonging' (Davis, 2024, p. 179).

[3] This argument has historical roots and also includes other groups of people not seen as mainstream taxpayers, e.g. both in gendered and in racial debates regarding taxation.

> The long history of taxpayer status in arguments shaping who gets to be a citizen and what the state must provide to realize the promise of full citizenship make clear that tax is inextricably bound up with a benefit/burden calculus that is not captured in the conventional tax understanding of benefit theory and that cannot be reduced to questions of administrability, efficiency, or equity measured by ability to pay. (Davis, 2024, p. 186)

We agree. Our focus is the UK with a very different taxation policy and administration of taxes from the USA, yet we also heard many reasonings that went beyond the longing for citizenship. We thus want to explore if going beyond citizenship can better be understood by thinking about belonging. Here we step away from citizenship on the basis that it doesn't adequately capture taxpaying practices. We find belonging to be a better link between fiscal contributions to the state, not necessarily replacing citizenship but rather enhancing it by bringing to the fore more emotional attachments.

Belonging

People have a profound need to belong (Axelrod, 1984; Elster, 1989). Fundamentally, a sense of belonging is not being alone. It is being or taking part in a group, a community, a society. Belonging creates a sense of sharing, of having something in common with groups of other people. Family and kin are usually the first groups a human belongs to—geographical territories the next (village/suburb/city, region, nation); as we grow up the number of groups proliferate based on religion, ideological beliefs, interests, friendships and others. Citizenship creates a feeling of belonging to a nation—of having common geographical borders, a shared history, the same passport, of being referred to by a common denomination (British!). You can create a sense of (formalised) belonging by applying to a club or an organisation, even by purchasing a membership of them.

A sense of belonging is a multidimensional concept, used in a wide range of contexts (Antonsich, 2010; Flick et al., 2019). Bhimji suggests that belonging 'encompasses citizenship, nationhood, gender, ethnicity and emotional dimensions of status or attachment' (2008, p. 414, cited in Antonsich, 2010).

Belonging has been defined as 'the process of creating a sense of identification with, or connection to, cultures, people, places and material objects' (May, 2013, p. 3, cited in Kemppainen et al., 2020).

Belonging is also about an emotional attachment, about 'feeling at home' (Yuval-Davis, 2011). Belonging is multifaceted. You can belong to many different groups simultaneously (Yuval-Davis, 2011) and these can be national, religious, ethnic, sexual, class, territorial or neighbourhood, etc. Nira Yuval-Davis proposes a differentiation between three major analytical facets in how people construct a sense of belonging. The first concerns social locations which are various categories to which a person is seen to belong. These are set categories and we understand it mainly from outsider perspectives as to whether it is race, ethnicity, gender or most commonly class. The locations are neither static nor mutually exclusive. A person can, for example, move through life from working class to middle. The second is identification and emotional attachment, which comes out of people's inner convictions. It entails 'embodied narratives' that are continuously in the making, connecting ideas about identity in the past, who I was, with wishful thinking about whom to be in the future, whom I want to be. This facet is both 'reflective and constitutive'. Finally, value systems concern a person's assessment of their perceived social location and identity attachment in relation to that of others in the group, in the community, in the nation.

A sense of belonging is mainly personal and individual, but communities and societies also see the need to make people feel that they belong. Governmental structures, organisations and networks often work explicitly to create social cohesion, commitment, loyalty, political order, etc. (Antonsich, 2010). It is a forceful strategy that can be used to create versatile workers (Vodopivec et al., 2019) or a powerful tool to create a sense of nationality (Anderson, 2006).

In the era of transnational migration, belonging has reappeared on the agenda (Antonsich, 2010). Thinking about belonging, for migrants, leads us to consider the question of integration and assimilation of migrants into the societies of their new home. Feelings of belonging might be a cultural artefact, an imagined sense of being part of a community or a nation (Anderson, 2006). A nation has both geographical/spatial and judicial boundaries with historical roots defining what it is, whereas a community is a more fleeting group distinguished empirically 'by the style in which they are imagined' (2006, p. 6). According to Anderson, such an imaginary reflects people's understanding of sharing values and views with a group of people they mostly do not know (even in the smallest nation you do not know most other members). The similarities that foster network building for migrants are based on not only ethnicity, but a wide variety including gender, parenting and shared political projects (Shubin, 2020). It may not be enough to have social networks, but successful agents also have 'the ability and disposition to use and sustain networks' (Thapar-Bjorkert & Sanghera, 2010, p. 247).

When a (new) sense of belonging is created, it becomes relational; it makes people consider what is important for them to feel at home, feel at ease, feel part of something, etc. Because feeling at home can essentially be made to contrast with what it means to be away from home (Hannerz, 2002).

As Kemppainen et al. (2020) observe, social and environmental changes may also trigger a sense of *not* belonging, leading to 'questioning the traditional customs and norms' (ibid., p. 799) of belonging. Similarly, exposure to negative images of migrants can lead to a desire to distance oneself from them, rather than challenge them, maybe by adopting a more cosmopolitan orientation and de-emphasise national origins (Quassoli & Dimitriadis, 2019). We find this in the UK context, as discussed in Chap. 3 under the heading of 'Ruptures'.

Accumulation of knowledge and experience of the host country's national culture by migrants can lead to a stronger sense of belonging, although 'going native' does not guarantee this, it is context dependent (Carruthers, 2002). For migrants, acceptance of overseas qualifications is not always straightforward.

Continued effort may be needed to maintain a sense of belonging, especially when the rules of the game change, for example, changes in citizenship regimes (Erel & Ryan, 2019). When migrants move to a new country, they may, or may not, fit with the host country; some migrants will be ill equipped to deal with the new social space in which they find themselves. As Reed-Danahay observes:

> Migrants bring their dispositions and worldviews with them—including ideas about presentation of self, understandings of neighborly reciprocity, and also a set of know-how, social connections, and skills (linguistic, social, educational) that may or may not be highly valued in the host setting. (2020, p. 132)

Reflections

Fiscal citizenship has proved to be a useful concept to shed light on the relation taxpayers might have with the governmental structure to which they pay tax. The concept of fiscal citizenship is complex and malleable. It can be thought of as having a political dimension, being used for political purposes. It can be thought of as intimately linked with a notion of social contract. It can also be thought of more narrowly as being compliant with tax obligations.

Citizenship is an element of belonging, but the terms are not equivalent. Although we can distinguish between formal and performative citizenship, our participants spoke rather about belonging when they related to being taxed and paying taxes. Belonging invoked a more emotional response and made taxpaying distinct from the technical and legal sense of citizenship. Citizenship was for these UK immigrants rather more practical; it was framed as the ability to work in response to political ruptures such as Brexit or maltreatment at border control.

Proposing belonging as another form of connectedness is a result of engaging with people 'in the wild'. We let migrants use their own words to describe their views on tax not using hitherto used tax research and analytical concepts. In the topography of academic disciplines, we were travellers who let those we met inform us on how they saw the landscape. The result of this engagement formed our belief that focusing too tightly on citizenship inhibits analysis because of the legal and formal connotations borne by the term. Yet, the fault is broader than pointing at legal formalities, because much tax scholarship has too narrowly used benefits theory and other economic reasoning to explain migrants' views on taxes. The notion of belonging may allow us to explore the many and varied sentiments people hold.

We come back to the nature of belonging in the context of fiscal contributions and reciprocity, fiscal belonging, in Chap. 4. Yet before we do that, we need to contextualise the reality in which our participants find themselves in the UK in 2021/22. We describe this context as a nexus of fields; how is tax policy created, what is taxed, how are taxes collected, what are they spent on and how are immigrants affected?

References

Anderson, B. 2006. *Imagined communities: Reflections on the origin and spread of nationalism*. Verso.

Antonsich, M. 2010. Searching for belonging—An analytical framework. *Geography Compass* 4:644–659.

Axelrod, R. 1984. *The evolution of co-operation*. Basic Books.

Bauder, H. 2008. Citizenship as capital: The distinction of migrant labor. *Alternatives* 33:315–333.

Bäumer Escobar, V. 2020. The fiscal commons tax evasion, the state, and commoning in a Catalonian cooperative. *Social Analysis* 64 (2): 59–78. https://doi.org/10.3167/sa.2020.640204.
Bhimji, F. 2008. Cosmopolitan belonging and diaspora: Second-generation British Muslim women travelling to South Asia. *Citizenship Studies* 12 (4): 413–427.
Björklund Larsen, L. 2017. *Shaping taxpayers. Values in action at the Swedish tax agency*. Oxford: Berghahn Books.
Boll, K. 2014. Shady car dealings and taxing work practices: An ethnography of a tax audit process. *Accounting, Organizations and Society* 39 (1): 1–19.
Burnyeat, G., and M. Sheild Johansson. 2022. An anthropology of the social contract: The political power of an idea. *Critique of Anthropology* 42 (3): 221–237.
Carruthers, A. 2002. The accumulation of national belonging in transnational fields: Ways of being at home in Vietnam. *Identities: Global Studies in Culture and Power* 9 (4): 423–444. https://doi.org/10.1080/10702890214872.
Davis, T. 2017. The tax-immigration nexus. *Denver Law Review* 94 (2): 195–254.
Davis, T. 2024. Taxation and belonging: The history and rhetoric of tax, full citizenship, and community membership in the United States. In *Taxation, citizenship and democracy in the 21st century*, ed. Y. Lind and R. S. Avi-Yonah, 169–186. Edward Elgar.
Dean, H. 2004. Popular discourse and the ethical deficiency of 'third way' conceptions of citizenship. *Citizenship Studies* 8 (1): 65–82.
Elster, J. 1989. *The cement of society: A study of social order*. Cambridge University Press.
Erel, U., and L. Ryan. 2019. Migrant capitals: Proposing a multi-level spatio-temporal analytical framework. *Sociology* 53 (2): 246–263. https://doi.org/10.1117/003038518785298.
Flick, U., A. Hirseland, and B. Hans. 2019. Walking and talking integration: Triangulation of data from interviews and go-alongs for exploring immigrant welfare recipients' sense(s) of belonging. *Qualitative Inquiry* 25 (8): 799–810.
Freund, A. 2019. Western corporate fiscal citizenship in the 21st century. *Northwestern Journal of International Law and Business* 40 (1): 123–156.
Guano, E. 2010. Taxpayers, thieves, and the state: Fiscal citizenship in contemporary Italy. *Ethnos Journal of Anthropology* 75 (4): 471–495.
Guyer, J. I. 1992. Representation without taxation: An essay on democracy in rural Nigeria, 1952-1990. *African Studies Review* 35 (1): 41–79. https://doi.org/10.2307/524445.
Hannerz, U. 2001. Introduktion: när fältet blir translokalt. In *Flera fält i ett. Socialantropologer om translokala fältstudier*, 7–35. Stockholm: Carlssons.
Hannerz, U. 2002. Where we are and who we want to be. In *The post national self: Belonging and identity*, ed. U. Hedetoft and M. E. Hjort, 217–232. University of Minnesota Press.

Isin, E. F., and B. S. Turner. 2007. Investigating citizenship: An agenda for citizenship studies. *Citizenship Studies* 11 (1): 5–17.
Kauppinen, A.-R. 2020. God's delivery state taxes, tithes, and a rightful return in urban Ghana. *Social Analysis* 64 (2): 35–58. https://doi.org/10.3167/sa.2020.640203.
Kemppainen, T., L. Kemppainen, H. Kuusio, S. Rask, and P. Saukkonen. 2020. Multifocal integration and marginalisation: A theoretical model and an empirical study on three immigrant groups. *Sociology* 54 (4): 782–805.
Killian, S., V. O'Regan, and P. O'Regan. 2023. "Uncomfortable territory": Personal and organisational values in the tax profession. *Accounting Forum* 47 (1): 1–23. https://doi.org/10.1080/01559982.2021.2004633.
Likhovski, A. 2017. *Tax law and social norms in mandatory Palestine and Israel.* Cambridge University Press.
Marcus, G. E. 1995. Ethnography in/of the world system: The emergence of multi-sited ethnography. *Annual Review of Anthropology* 24:95–117.
Marshall, T.H. (2013 [1950]). Citizenship and social class. In S. Lazar (Ed.) *The anthropology of citizenship. A reader.* Wiley Blackwell.
Martin, I. W., Ajay Mehrotra, and M. Prasad. 2010. *New fiscal sociology: Taxation in comparative and historical perspective.* Cambridge University Press.
May, V. 2013. *Connecting self to society: Belonging in a changing world.* Macmillan.
Mehrotra, A. K. 2015. Reviving fiscal citizenship. *Michigan Law Review* 113 (6): 943–972.
Mehrotra, A. K. 2017. Fiscal forearms: Taxation as the lifeblood of the modern fiscal state. In *The many hands of the state: Theorizing the complexities of political authority and social control*, ed. K. Morgan and A. Orloff, 17–34. Cambridge University Press.
Morgen, S., and J. Erickson. 2017. Incipient 'commoning' in defense of the public? Competing varieties of fiscal citizenship in tax- and spending-related direct democracy. *Focaal: Journal of Global and Historical Anthropology* 79:54–66. https://doi.org/10.3167/fcl.2017.790105.
Mulligan, E., and L. Oats. 2016. Tax professionals at work in Silicon Valley. *Accounting, Organizations and Society* 52:63–76. https://doi.org/10.1016/j.Aos.2015.09.005.
Musgrave, R. A. 1997. Reconsidering the fiscal role of government. *The American Economic Review* 87 (2): 156–159.
Oats, L. 2012. Tax as a social and institutional practice. In *Taxation: A fieldwork research handbook*, ed. L. Oats, 3–8. Routledge.
Ong, A. 1999. *Flexible citizenship: The cultural logics of transnationality.* Duke University Press.
Ormeno-Pèrez, R., and L. Oats. 2023. Implementing problematic tax regulation: Hysteresis and bureaucratic revolutionaries within tax administrations. *The British Accounting Review* 55 (3): 101147. https://doi.org/10.1016/j.bar.2022.101147.

Quassoli, F., and I. Dimitriadis. 2019. 'Here, there, in between, beyond …' identity negotiation and sense of belonging among southern Europeans in the UK and Germany. *Social Inclusion* 7 (4): 60–70.

Reed-Danahay, D. 2020. Brexit, liminality, and ambiguities of belonging. French citizens in London. *Ethnologia Europaea* 50 (2): 16–31.

Rogers, H., and L. Oats. 2022. Transfer pricing: Changing views in changing times. *Accounting Forum* 46 (1): 83–107.

Roitman, J. L. 2005. *Fiscal disobedience: An anthropology of economic regulation in Central Africa*. Princeton: Princeton University Press.

Schmidt, C., and E. Matthaei. 2024. Conceptualising fiscal citizenship. In *Taxation citizenship and democracy in the 21st century*, ed. Y. Lind and R. Avi Yonah, 53–81. Elgar.

Shield Johansson, M. 2020. Taxes for independence rejecting a fiscal model of reciprocity in peri-urban Bolivia. *Social Analysis* 64 (2): 18–37. https://doi.org/10.3167/sa.2020.640202.

Shubin, S. 2020. Evaluating the process of cross-European migration: Beyond cultural capital. *Transactions of the Institute of British Geographers* 45 (4): 802–816.

Sparrow, J. T. 2008. Buying our boys back': The mass foundations of fiscal citizenship in World War II. *Journal of Policy History* 20 (2): 263–286.

Thapar-Bjorkert, S., and G. Sanghera. 2010. Social capital, educational aspirations and young Pakistani Muslim men and women in Bradford, West Yorkshire. *The Sociological Review* 58 (2): 244–264.

Tjernberg, M. 2010. The economy of undocumented migration: Taxation and access to welfare. *European Journal of Migration and Law* 12 (2): 149–171. https://doi.org/10.1163/157181610X496858.

Twine, F. 1994. *Citizenship and social rights: The interdependence of self and society*. SAGE.

Vicol, D. 2023. Into and out of citizenship through personal tax payments: Romanian migrants' leveraging of British self-employment. In *Beyond the social contract: An anthropology of tax*, ed. N. Makovicky and R. Smith, 101–119. Berghahn Books.

Vodopivec, M., D. Finn, S. Laporšek, M. Vodopivec, and N. Cvörnjek. 2019. Increasing employment of older workers: Addressing labour market obstacles. *Journal of Population Ageing* 12 (3): 273–298. https://doi.org/10.1007/s12062-018-9236-4.

Wynter, C., and L. Oats. 2018. Don't worry, we are not after you! Anancy culture and tax enforcement in Jamaica. *Critical Perspectives on Accounting* 57:56–69. https://doi.org/10.1016/j.cpa.2018.01.004.

Yuval-Davis, N. 2011. *The politics of belonging: Intersectional contestations*. Sage.

CHAPTER 3

The UK Context

Abstract It is important to appreciate the context in which ethnographic fieldwork (or any other form of research) takes place. This chapter describes the prevailing conditions at the time of our fieldwork. Both politics and fiscal matters have low salience in Britain and our participants describe their lack of knowledge of tax. The fiscal field is that part of public policy that deals with both raising government funds through taxes and spending. As immigrants they face particular difficulties, compounded by their status which can be uncertain due to shifting immigration policies and ruptures in the immigration field.

Keywords UK tax system • HMRC • Public policy • The fiscal field

It is not only tax that matters in the world, so does context. Although the fieldwork that inspired our development of the concept of fiscal belonging took place largely in the UK, we draw to some extent on fieldwork from other countries in the fiscal citizenship project, specifically Canada and Germany. As noted in the previous chapter, we believe it is important to contextualise fieldwork—to be aware of the prevailing social, economic, cultural and political conditions when the data was collected. This chapter describes the UK context at the time of the fieldwork, mainly between June 2021 and December 2021, reflecting also on historical events

L. Björklund Larsen, L. Oats, *Crossing Borders, Sharing Burdens*,
https://doi.org/10.1007/978-3-031-99394-7_3

leading up to that context, in particular those that clearly resonated with our participants.

Our primary concern in this book is fiscal belonging, as an adjunct to the more commonly discussed fiscal citizenship. We see the 'fiscal' in fiscal belonging in the British context as comprising collection of revenue by government in the form of taxes, but importantly also the spending of funds by government in the provision of services to society. Both of these facets of the fiscal field are aspects of public policy and interact with and are influenced by adjacent fields. We first explore the relevant adjacent fields before coming back to an understanding of what we call the fiscal field in the UK context. We then turn to issues of migration. Our participants are all immigrants, and all were or had been resident in England, and so we describe the field of UK immigration, including citizenship to help better understand how they describe their experiences of and attitudes towards tax and benefits in the UK.

The concept of 'field' is powerful in social sciences and yet is used by scholars in different ways and for different purposes. In Chap. 2 we discussed how the concept of field is important to our methodology, defining among whom we conduct our fieldwork and the relevant context. In this chapter we use the concept of field in a slightly different way, as a conceptual tool for organising a broad discussion of the context in which our fieldwork took place.

Field theory is not a unified theory, but rather best thought of as a family of theories with a common thread.[1] Martin (2003, p. 1) describes field theory as 'a more or less coherent approach …whose essence is the explanation of regularities in individual action by recourse to position vis a vis others'. In the same way that conducting fieldwork requires an understanding of the field in which it takes place, what is important in field

[1] Martin (2003) traces field theory in the social sciences from its origins in the traditional physical sciences and focuses on three main directions of travel. First is Lewin's (1951) social psychological theory which argued that behaviour should be defined as a function of both personality and environment. Second is Pierre Bourdieu's field theory that sees a field as a social space or area of activity in which there is constant struggle between actors seeking dominance through the accumulation of physical and symbolic resources conferring power (see Bourdieu & Wacquant, 1992 for an introduction). Third is field theory associated with DiMaggio and Powell and used in organisation studies to capture interorganisational behaviour (1983). To this list can be added Fligstein and McAdam (2012) who see fields as spaces where strategic action takes place (e.g. De Widt & Oats, 2024).

theory is that the capacity and actions of actors cannot be understood without also understanding the dynamics of the field itself.

Many scholars use the concept of field without adopting a particular strand of field theory. It is often used as a substitute for arena, sphere or space. As Kauppi (2018) notes, it is taken to mean 'an organised social space with rules, institutions and actors' so as to simplify social reality in order to make it more manageable.

In this chapter, we use a loose conception of 'field' but draw on what we see as the common threads of the different strands of field theory, which is based on the idea that societies are made up of different spheres that can be thought of as fields. These fields are not 'real things'; they are analytical tools used by researchers to better understand the phenomenon being studied. Fields are not independent of one another and sometimes what we designate as a field may overlap with, or be nested within, other fields, there are potentially any number of fields and how they are conceptualised depends on the object of study—the puzzle that is being investigated. Each field has its own logic or ways of thinking that guides both its internal operation and its relationships with other fields. Importantly, fields are not static; they may change over time, sometimes in response to new developments or external shocks including changes in associated fields. Actors inhabit many different fields at any one time and experience being within fields differently. In some fields actors may be comfortable and able to fit, understanding the field's logic and contributing to the field's ongoing existence. In other fields, actors may feel uncomfortable and out of place, maybe through not understanding the logic of the field. At times also, a change in a field will lead to an actor who was previously comfortable to become uncomfortable.

We are particularly concerned with public policy: decisions that are made by governments about how we live our lives and which can be thought of as comprising two distinct fields: the political field in which government policy decisions are made and the bureaucratic field in which government policy is put into operation. Within these fields all manner of public policies are devised and implemented but one particular object of public policy is at the core of this book: the field of fiscal policy, which we see as comprising two distinct activities, taxing and spending. We then consider the position of migrants, by reference to another field of public policy, immigration.

The Political Field

The political field is where political actors debate and create public policy, representing social interests and enacting left and right ideologies.

For many years the UK has operated as a two-party system with the Conservatives (blue/right) and Labour (red/left) dominant in elections and able to hold power for long periods of time. The system has sometimes been called 'my turn, your turn', with very limited scope for insurgent new parties to gain traction. Right and left in the UK context differs from other countries in that the tendency is towards the centre; indeed it could be said that there are no extreme or 'far' right and left parties. The 'centre' is probably to the left of, say, that in the USA. The 'first past the post' system allows the political party with the highest number of votes to form a government, with the leader of the winning party assuming the role of Prime Minister, supported by the Cabinet. Parliamentary business is adversarial, often with heated debates. There is one official opposition party which leads the challenges to the governing party's policies. The extent to which the opposition is successful in changing the course of legislation depends on the size of the majority of Members of Parliament (MPs) held by the party in power. Parliament is responsible for legislation and for authorising the government's plans for both spending and revenue raising.

General elections are generally held every five years, and in late 2021, the Conservative government had been in power for 11 years, the first five of which were in coalition with the Liberal Democrats. In 2015 the Conservatives secured a majority of MPs in the general election, followed by a reduced majority in the 2017 snap general election and then with a large majority in Parliament following the general election in 2019 when Boris Johnson became Prime Minister. Although the period following Johnson's subsequent resignation in 2022 was turbulent, at the time of our fieldwork, there was relative stability in government, albeit with considerable fractures and dissatisfaction over the handling of the Covid-19 pandemic.

Politics generally has low salience among the UK public and the level of commitment to one or other of the two main political parties has been on the wane for some time. Voting is not compulsory and in the 2019 general election around 67% of the electorate cast votes. The two-party 'squeeze' meant that minor parties were not able to secure a significant number of MPs, and in England, Conservatives and Labour together secured over

98% of the seats with 81% of the votes. The Liberal Democrats were disadvantaged by the first past the post system.

Between 1972 and 2020 the UK was a member of the European Union (EU) and in the intervening years European law had a significant influence on the UK legal system. The decision to leave the EU was the result of a referendum held in 2016 which was won by a narrow majority of voters following a divisive campaign which polarised 'leavers' and 'remainers'. A new political party, UKIP, was formed with its main platform of exiting the EU, but it failed to secure any seats in the 2019 general election. Brexit is an important rupture in the political field—one that resonated with our participants as will be seen later, under the heading of 'ruptures'.

The ideological convergence of the two main political parties in the UK, away from extreme left and right and towards the centre, has reinforced the symbolic domination of what is sometimes referred to as the 'Westminster bubble', a derogatory term to denote the detachment of politicians and policymakers from the lived lives of the majority of the electorate, leading to an anti-politics sentiment (Stanley, 2018).

The Bureaucratic Field

The bureaucratic field is a relatively autonomous space, meaning that it is relatively free from political interference, which is constituted positively for the public good and negatively through denial of private interests (Demenge & Robert, 2024). By thinking of it in terms of a field, we can move away from thinking of the state as being monolithic and homogeneous. Here we are concerned with that part of the bureaucratic field that is concerned with the practicalities of fiscal matters, i.e. implementing taxing and spending policies.

The British civil service has a reputation for professionalism and neutrality in terms of political affiliation, built over a long period of time, although called into question more recently in the face of various shocks such as Brexit and the Covid-19 pandemic. Although central to government in the UK, the civil service does not have a clear identity or defined responsibilities and accountability (Thomas et al., 2022).

The administrative machinery comprises departments dealing with specific areas of expertise such as tax, immigration and security. Since the Thatcher era, there have been shifts in the way in which the civil service operates with increasing use of targets, outsourcing and an emphasis on professional management, i.e. embrace of new public management techniques (Thomas et al., 2022).

Throughout government there has been a clear attempt in recent decades to reshape the way services are provided, with privatisation and choice being embraced by both main political parties, which can be traced back to the Thatcher Conservative government which shifted UK policy towards a neoliberal model, subsequently embraced by the Blair/Brown Labour government. The onus is on citizens to identify their own needs and act on these, in contrast with earlier models that were top down, state led. This model of public service provision entails a neoliberal logic of individualisation and market logic, in particular assuming that citizens are free to choose better services and have equal capacity in the market.

Public Policy

Richard Rose (1987) describes the metaphorical state in which there is one tiller but two pairs of hands steering, one being party politicians (in the political field) and the other being higher civil servants (in the bureaucratic field). This is not necessarily a comfortable relationship and government policy development and implementation frequently entails power struggles. In theory, ministers appointed by the Prime Minister are the decision-makers and civil servants advise on and implement those decisions. The civil service, however, has the power to constrain policy change where it conflicts with civil service ethos and/or capabilities.

The spaces of public policy are occupied by agents with varied professional affiliations, and therefore presumed expertise, which lend them legitimacy through titles such as lawyer, judge, economist and inspector. Expertise is particularly important in the field of public policy. Politicians are faced with information gaps; they cannot possibly be expert in all aspects of government policy. Ministers are therefore reliant on advice, advised by special advisers (known as spads), whose role includes bridging the gap between politicians and the civil service. Spads are temporary civil servants who report to an individual minister and undertake a variety of duties including commenting on written submission from officials to ministers (Hillman, 2014). Economic expertise plays a large role in UK public policy and economists are embedded throughout the bureaucratic field, in line with the depiction of economics as vegetation in our topography, some welcome, some not.

Demands on public policy are constantly shifting. Longer-term trends include demographic changes such that by 2022 the British population is 'older, more ethnically diverse, more educated and less religious' than it was four decades earlier, leading to a liberalisation of moral attitudes (Clery, 2023). Public policy responds to these changes, but in turn shapes them.

The UK Fiscal Field

For the purposes of this book, we focus our attention on two broad areas of public policy: tax collection and public spending, which together form what we call the fiscal field. This chimes with Pierre Bourdieu's idea of two hands of the state, the left encompassing the ministries in charge of social functions (education, health, housing) and the right 'charged with enforcing the new economic discipline via budget cuts, fiscal incentives and economic deregulation' (Wacquant, 2015). In the UK, tax is most often thought of as an economic phenomenon and changes in tax practices respond to changes in the economy. Public spending is also dependent on the robustness of the economy. The overall tax and benefit system in the UK is redistributive. In one report, the poorest 40% of the population was found to receive more in cash benefits from the government than they pay in taxes (Keep, 2023).

The UK is one of the more fiscally centralised countries among Western economies, notwithstanding devolution that has granted fiscal powers to Scotland and Wales. Local governments in all regions are dependent on central government funding and have constrained revenue raising powers despite heavy burdens in terms of social spending provision.

Both parts of the UK fiscal field discussed below were affected significantly by the Covid-19 pandemic. When our interviews took place, Covid-19 Omicron variant was still circulating, although generalised restrictions were mostly ended before our interviews. The UK response included joint working between His Majesty's Treasury (hereafter the Treasury) and His Majesty's Revenue and Customs (HMRC) to provide financial support through various schemes including temporary tax easements, e.g. to defer payment of value added tax (VAT), self-employed grants, additional payments to working tax credits households and tax relief for people working from home.[2] The provision of public financial support was probably the reason for the surprisingly positive attitude towards tax that participants held.

Taxing

Tax policy is largely controlled by the Treasury drawing on a narrow range of expertise (mainly economic) from within and outside of government (including professional tax bodies). Having said that, tax policy is influenced by a plethora of actors including expert practitioners, lobby groups and professional associations. The central tax system is administered by HMRC, although it has input into the detailed working of high-level policy formulated by Treasury officials. The superficial separation of functions between these two departments is dysfunctional to the extent that it allows both to disclaim accountability. Arguably, both departments are insular and opaque, rarely engaging in wide consultation, despite the introduction of a formal process for tax policymaking in 2010.[3] The relation between government ministers and civil servants in HMRC is distant, underlining HMRC's relative autonomy within the fiscal field (Tuck et al., 2019).

There is no formal tax strategy to inform policy development. Importantly, the two main parties have begun to converge on the question of the tax burden. Labour is traditionally the party of high tax burdens, directed primarily at wealthier members of society. Conservative policy leans towards lower tax burdens. Yet while in government, each party deviated from this overall ethos, most recently with the Conservatives, in the wake of Covid-19, presiding over high levels of tax burden. A trend emerged in the 2000s towards 'hiding' tax increases among the complexity of the UK tax system. These so-called stealth taxes, including holding

[2] As of May 2021 the Coronavirus Job Retention Scheme provided £61.3 billion to 1.3 million employers, the Self Employment Income Support Scheme provided £19.7 billion to some 7.1 million claimants and the Eat out to Help Out scheme paid out £849.2 million to support the hospitality industry. See https://civilservice.blog.gov.uk/2021/05/25/how-hmrc-and-hmt-delivered-coronavirus-support-schemes-together/

[3] There has concern raised that the government does not always adhere to this policymaking process; for example, for a House of Commons Treasury Committee inquiry into tax after Coronavirus in 2021, see https://committees.parliament.uk/work/465/tax-after-coronavirus/publications/

tax thresholds steady to create fiscal drag,[4] further add to the complexity of the tax system which has ramifications for both administration and compliance.

Civil servants in the Treasury and HMRC play a pivotal role in translating government policy ideas into proposals capable of practical implementation. For some years now it has been accepted that the Treasury controls tax policy, and HMRC manages administration. In practice HMRC feeds into policy decisions through both a formal agreement[5] and informal channels.

There is no systematic review of tax legislation and evaluation as to effectiveness is patchy. That part of the bureaucratic field that deals with tax, primarily HMRC, is protected from political interference by being a non-ministerial department. It has considerable autonomy, and when administrative decisions and actions are called into question by, for example, parliamentary committees or the National Audit Office (NAO), HMRC is able to refuse information on the grounds of confidentiality, which forms part of the (largely) unchallenged logic of the field.

The UK Tax System in Overview

Tax, like politics, has low salience in the UK. As Rosie, originating in Scandinavia, observes, 'it's talked about more in Scandinavia and people are more aware of it. The people like, you'd get comments more about that taxes are high or that. Yeah, people, people kind of discuss it more than here. Here it is, nobody really discusses it. It just is'.

While tax policy is a political battleground, especially during the lead up to elections, the level of understanding of the tax system among politicians, the commentariat and the public generally is arguably poor. Specific issues catch the attention of the media from time to time, but most usually, public debate is confined to the financial press and technical

[4] The term fiscal drag refers to the freezing of tax rate thresholds so that taxpayers are moved into higher tax brackets purely as a result of inflation. The UK has for many years adjusted income tax thresholds to prevent this impact.

[5] There is a policy partnership agreement between HMRC and the Treasury that is described as a key relationship in the design and delivery of tax policy. The partnership is carefully managed in terms of information sharing including imposing a duty of confidentiality on Treasury officials who spend time in HMRC and vice versa; see HMRC Internal Manual Information Disclosure Guide IDG52200 available at https://www.gov.uk/hmrc-internal-manuals/information-disclosure-guide/idg52200#:~:text=The%20policy%20partnership%20between%20HMRC,delivery%20of%20existing%20tax%20policy.

publications (e.g. tax practitioner journals and magazines). So what does the UK tax system look like?

Income tax is the most important source of revenue for the UK. It is imposed on individuals at progressive rates with savings and dividends being taxed more lightly than other forms of income. Income from employment and self-employment are also subject to national insurance contributions. The first £12,570 of income is exempted from tax, after which income tax is at 20%, 40% and 45%. Around 60% of adults have income high enough to pay income tax.[6]

Taxpayers paying the highest rate of income tax contribute nearly 40% of income tax revenue. When asked about what taxes they paid, all of our participants mentioned income tax, and some also national insurance contributions. The PAYE system of income tax withholding for employees means that for most taxpayers, the monthly payslip is a regular visible reminder of income tax and national insurance payments. Taxpayers within the 20% income tax band and without other sources of income are generally not required to file a tax return. Katie, born in Eastern Europe, when asked about what taxes she pays, says, 'To be honest, I feel so bad. I actually don't know. And I would say like I don't care in a way. Right. Because it's being taken out automatically'.

For those not in employment, tax is largely visible twice yearly, in July when a prepayment is made towards the year's tax liability and at the end of January when the tax return is filed and liability is finalised, although HMRC are in the process of introducing digital reporting on a more regular basis. Self-employed taxpayers are more lightly taxed than employees, paying a lower rate of national insurance contribution, and especially when employers' national insurance contributions (essentially a payroll tax) are taken into account. Corporation tax is complex for small companies. Rosie says that she stopped working for her own company and became an employee again:

> I found the whole side about taxes so extremely stressful. And it took up so much of my time just to understand what I needed to do to make sure everything was legal. And I was so scared I would do something that wasn't correct, which I need to do everything correctly. It is just my personality. I could not make a mistake. So yes that really stressed me out to the point that

[6] The devolved Scottish government has the power to set its own rates of income tax and they differ slightly from these.

> still, when I think about taxes, it stresses me out, even though I know I'm paying them and everything's fine.

After income tax and national insurance, the next biggest contributor to national tax revenue is VAT. Very few of our participants mentioned VAT as one of the taxes they paid. This may be because VAT is not as visible as equivalent consumption taxes in other countries. There are a plethora of other indirect taxes including those on alcohol and tobacco, fuel duties and a number of environmental taxes. Interestingly, one of our participants specifically mentioned the TV licence, which is not usually described as a tax, as it is hypothecated to fund the British Broadcasting Corporation (BBC).

A separate capital gains tax applies to the profit on disposal of assets, and stamp duty is imposed on transactions in property based on its value. Inheritance tax is becoming increasingly intrusive and has gone from a tax that affected only the very wealthy to wider coverage, largely because the threshold at which it comes into effect has been held at the same value for several years, while property values have increased.

Several of our participants mentioned council tax, which is a local government tax based on property value. This is one area where taxpayers call into question the value they get. Rosie, for example, says, 'I'm not seeing it. So I'm just wondering where is that money going? How is it being spread and used and monitor it? So I don't think that it's being administered properly, so I get a little bit upset about that. But what can I do?'

HMRC: Tax Administration

As the body in charge of administering the central tax system, HMRC is a dominant player in the practices of the tax collection side of fiscal field. The guiding principles of HMRC include a commitment to neutrality, i.e. distance from political interference and ideological influences, as well as equality of treatment of taxpayers regardless of background, activities, size or other distinguishing characteristics. A conscious shift away from equality of treatment can be seen in recent years with increased compliance control activities that are informed by and draw on behavioural science (nudge) techniques which target particular types of taxpayers and treat them differently in pursuit of the overall goal of 'closing the tax gap'. Arun Advani (2022) analyses HMRC data to establish who does and does not pay tax and finds the largest single tax gap is from taxpayers who file self-assessment tax returns.

HMRC's ethos is 'imbued with notions of service to society, and processes are controlled to secure equitable treatment across the taxpayer population' (Gracia & Oats, 2012, p. 309). Technical mastery of HMRC's view of the tax law is important and internal manuals are made publicly available so there is transparency around how HMRC believes the tax law operates in practice.

HMRC, like other government departments, has embraced new public management, essentially requiring operations to be run consistent with private sector principles, assumed to be more efficient than 'old style' bureaucratic principles. As part of this, taxpayers were rebranded as 'customers' (Tuck, 2013), to be treated as such. HMRC has, however, been repeatedly criticised for poor 'customer' service, for example, by parliamentary committees and the National Audit Office (NAO). HMRC has expended considerable resources to improve customer service, including conducting customer satisfaction surveys and, in 2022, a 'brand' study to assess how the public perceive HMRC and have confidence and trust in the organisation.

Taxpayers' attitudes towards paying tax emerges from their experiences and interactions within the tax field as part of the wider fiscal field. On the whole UK taxpayers generally have high compliance with the tax rules (Gracia & Oats, 2012). Several of our participants mentioned problems in their dealings with HMRC that reinforce the view that customer service is not as good as it should be. The main criticism is inaccessibility, in terms of both the provision of advice and the availability and poor quality of guidance. The inability to find someone to talk to was frustrating, 'it's difficult to get through … if you want to ask', says Colin, born and raised in Southern Europe. According to Alison, originating in a Nordic country, 'if you want to talk, it takes ages … you can't see anyone, you never see anyone. Everything is online or there is a voice—press one, press two, we play a little music for you while you are just sitting in the queue'.

Alison observed 'no one told me you have to figure it out yourself … the information is not accessible … it's a complicated language'. Denise also finds the tax system inaccessible: 'to me, it sometimes feels like it's all designed. I mean, it sounds a little bit cynical, but it can sometimes feel like it's designed to be intimidating and even though you know I'm an educated person ... I don't have problems understanding most things. I find it quite inaccessible'. Confidentiality of taxpayer information is also vigorously protected by HMRC, an issue she found puzzling having come from Scandinavia where there is much greater transparency. She goes on to say: 'the language, the way it all works there, they're not very easy to get hold of, if you'd have to ask a question … here it feels like they're not speaking to the kind of commoner, the average person. It feels like they're speaking to people who know what they're doing and understand it'.

Katie echoes the sentiments, saying, 'I just feel like whenever I try and find any information on the government website, sometimes it's just very confusing, sometimes I read advice on the gov.uk page. For whatever reason, I'm like, I've got no clue what I'm supposed to do or I don't know what this is because it's like a British-ism or something like that'. Rosie is critical of HMRC call centres, saying 'they could have … more people in their call centres actually answer questions, you know, have actual humans you can talk to. They don't have enough and it takes hours to get through to someone. And then, yeah, they're not always very helpful'.

The principle of equal treatment was brought into question in relation to allegations of letting multinationals get away with not paying a fair share of taxes. This was fuelled by the commentariat who shone a spotlight on the issue from around 2012 and was commented on by several of our participants. Writing in 2013, Richard Brooks suggests that the tax system had been captured by the tax industry and further that 'policy is determined through committees and consultation processes in which the tax avoidance industry's representatives dominate, before being nodded through parliament without proper debate' (2013, p. 290). One of our interviewees, Denise, notes the influence of the media, remarking 'it's so hard to know if it's kind of headlines that you read, but the feeling definitely the very richest in society don't contribute their fair share'. In one study of HMRC practices at the other end of the scale, tax credit claimants, it is suggested that neoliberal values dominate with adverse impacts on both workers and citizens (Closs-Davies et al., 2020).

Spending

Stanley (2018) suggests that there is an increasing gap between what people expect regarding tax and spending. He reports evidence of 'the actual lived experiences of engaging with the uses and abuses of taxpayers money' leads him to conclude that the tax morale of British taxpayers is declining. While the focus of our work is willingness to pay tax, the issue of reciprocity arose consistently in our interviews and so it is appropriate to outline the UK position in relation to welfare spending. The UK welfare system is based on the post-WWII principles designed to ensure that every person has access to healthcare, education, employment and support when poor throughout their lives.

In terms of public spending, the welfare system is the largest component of cash transfers from the government. O'Grady (2022) charts the transformation of welfare policy observing a significant shift in both discourse and policy in relation to welfare recipients. He notes that the British public have turned against welfare recipients more than in other countries, although policy is not dictated by public opinion. However, in addition, the field of public service provision is unevenly distributed and arguably favours the middle classes over the poorer in society (Hastings & Matthews, 2015). The majority of welfare benefit claimants do not need a record of national insurance contributions or income tax payments.

Universal credit was introduced in 2010 to deal with the dysfunctional aspects of the previous system that included a myriad of different benefits with differing entitlement rules with some recipients eligible for benefits from different programmes. It is administered by the Department of Work and Pensions (DWP), whereas the tax credit system was administered by HMRC. At the time of our research, one study found that 54.2% of individuals lived in households that received more in benefits then they paid in taxes, the highest 'net dependency ratio' on record (Knox & Lilley, 2023).

Overall, the tax and benefit system is redistributive in that better off households pay more in taxes than they receive in benefits and vice versa for the less well off. Income inequality, as measured by the Gini Coefficient, was at 29.9% in 2020/21, having fallen from a peak of 33.8% in 2007/08 (Knox & Lilley, 2023).

One point of overlap between tax and public spending is the provision of tax reliefs. Tax reliefs, or tax expenditures, result from policy decisions to refrain from taxing particular activities or classes of taxpayer. The UK makes extensive use of tax reliefs which provide benefits, primarily to the middle classes, but remains largely opaque and lacking accountability. Recent investigations into tax reliefs by the NAO reveal a proliferation of reliefs that are not monitored or evaluated, unlike direct public spending (NAO, 2020).

The Immigration Field

Our study of fiscal belonging concentrates on immigrants. All of our participants live, or have lived, in the UK, specifically England. The final part of this exploration of the UK context therefore relates to immigrants. There is very little interaction between the fiscal field and the immigration field, although both are part of the wider public policy field. The latter has been very turbulent in recent years following Brexit and spanning the Covid-19 pandemic.

The UK 2021 census[7] found that one in six usual residents of England and Wales were born outside the UK, an increase since 2011 from 13.4% to 16.8%. India is the most common country of birth outside the UK, followed by Poland and Pakistan. Of the residents in England and Wales born outside of the UK, 42.4% had arrived before 2011, 26.9% had arrived between 2001 and 2010 and 30.7% had arrived before 2001.

The UK's immigration system has 'long been characterised by restrictive policies, absurdly complex and ever-changing Immigration Rules, harsh and arbitrary decision making, criminalisation of mobility and indefinite immigration detention' (Griffiths & Yeo, 2021, by reference to Goodfellow, 2019). However, migration to the UK as a percentage of the population has been high by international standards in recent decades and has driven population growth. The UK does not have a central population database or identity card system and data on immigration is apparently incomplete or even inaccurate.

Acquiring Citizenship

The backdrop for the decision whether and when to apply for citizenship is constantly changing. Prabhat (2019, p. xii) notes: '[M]ost rights to British citizenship arise from a combination of birth and descent or through long-term presence (naturalisation). As there is no single determinative factor in acquiring citizenship there is much confusion about who can become British and, indeed, how they can do so … the political rhetoric surrounding citizenship is high octane'. Citizenship does not

[7] See https://www.ons.gov.uk/peoplepopulationandcommunity/populationandmigration/internationalmigration/bulletins/internationalmigrationenglandandwales/census2021

actually provide much legal protection; indeed long-term residency confers more security (ibid.).

Immigrants seek British citizenship for various reasons. A British passport facilitates easier identification and travel, which may be a primary motivation for some immigrants. For others, applying for citizenship will provide confirmation of a commitment to stay in Britain (Byrne, 2019).

All migrants are subject to the visa system, which defines their rights to live and work in the UK. Once a migrant has been in the UK for five years, they will usually be eligible to apply for Indefinite Leave to Remain (ILR) which allows individuals to live and work freely in the UK. Once the individual has been granted ILR and has been resident in the UK for another 12 months, they are eligible to apply for UK citizenship. Interestingly, British citizenship does not require active demonstration of loyalty although there is a citizenship test. The current test is the third edition which was launched in 2013. Brooks (2019) is critical of all editions of the test. In relation to the third edition, he argues that it is now less helpful in terms of providing practical information such as how to claim benefits. There are a number of barriers to achieving naturalisation, not least of which is a substantial fee (see Harvey, 2019). There is also evidence that migrants from poorer countries are less likely to pass the citizenship tests, as are those from countries where the main language is not English (van Oers, 2014, p. 183, cited in Prabhat, 2018).

Belonging in Britain

Yuval-Davis describes 'political projects of belonging', that is, attempts by the state to foster integration by migrants, for example, the citizenship test. These political projects are aimed at constructing boundaries as well as articulating an 'essence of Britishness'. As Prabhat (2018, p. 15) notes, '[T]he "imagined community" of the British state is one that consists of the majority ethnic citizenry and its values', although as she goes on to state, the search for British values can be likened to the search for the Holy Grail, consensus is hard to find and majority values become a proxy for all. Examples of Britishness provided by Prabhat's interviewees include tea drinking, strawberries and cream, cricket, love of dogs, politeness and respect for rules and beer.

Prabhat found the word 'belong' came up a lot in her interviews about citizenship, as did we when we started our Fiscal Citizenship project fieldwork. She notes that people can have a strong sense of belonging without legal status; conversely that legal status does not ensure a sense of belonging and also that time is the most relevant factor for developing a sense of belonging—'people construct belonging through interactions and this takes place over time as they become more acquainted with their new country' (p. 51). A number of her interviewees sought citizenship for the benefit of their children's sense of belonging rather than their own. Some migrants from former colonies have an inherited sense of Britishness from parents or grandparents with a strong Commonwealth identity. Many come to feel British long before naturalising, although the difficult process of obtaining citizenship can 'sometimes chip away at "Britishness"' (Prabhat, 2018, p. 76).

A report published in 2021[8] found that Britain ranks highly in Europe as a leader in social cohesion and economic fairness, especially over matters of race, outperforming white majority, multi-ethnic European countries such as France, Germany and the Netherlands when it comes to anti-discrimination legislation (Eshan, 2023). The UK has some of the strongest equalities bodies in the world; nonetheless, there are well-documented problems with parallel communities in certain parts of England.[9] Indeed migrants vary in terms of their openness to embracing Britishness and the extent to which they bring their past lives with them, which may mark them out as different, making belonging more difficult.

Ruptures

From time to time, events occur that shake up feelings of attachment to Britain. Such field changes can cause disruption leading to feeling like a fish out of water. Four issues in particular were prominent in the news in the run up to our fieldwork. The first is the hostile environment created in 2012, the second is the Windrush scandal, the third is the revocation of the British citizenship of Shamima Begum and the fourth was Brexit. We bring these specific events up as they were referred to by our participants.

[8] Commission on Race and Ethnic Disparities (2021), 'Commission on Race and Ethnic Disparities: The Report', March. Available at: https://assets.publishing.service.gov.uk/government/uploads/system/uploads/attachment_data/file/974507/20210331_-_CRED_Report_-_FINAL_-_Web_Accessible.pdf

[9] According to the Migrant Integration Policy Index 2020, cited in Esham 2023.

The Hostile Environment

The so-called hostile environment was created in 2012 under Theresa May's tenure as Home Secretary and represented a step change, 'unprecedented in the UK in its scale, scope and speed' (Griffiths & Yeo, 2021, p. xx). An important element of the 'hostile environment' is its fragmentation and the co-option of private sector actors into the realm of immigration control, described by Griffiths and Yeo (2021) as 'deputisation'. The emergence and sedimentation of the 'hostile environment' saw a range of third parties becoming responsible for monitoring the immigration status of people under their control and in their care—landlords, banks, educational institutions, the drivers' licence authorities, marriage registrars and public health organisations. Two Immigration Acts, in 2014 and 2016, together with various secondary legislation have considerably expanded the reach of immigration governance in the UK.

A notable part of the suite of initiatives that collectively comprise the 'hostile environment' was Operation Vaken, a communications pilot developed by the Home Office and put into operation in 2013. Included in the campaign were 'ad vans', designed to encourage immigration offenders to depart the UK voluntarily by increasing awareness. Home Office operational intelligence suggested that offenders made aware of the voluntary departure route were more likely to avail themselves of it. The 'ad vans' were mobile billboards that set out how many arrests there had been in the most recent week and offered a contact number for advice. Operation Vaken lasted for one month and the subsequent evaluation was inconclusive as to its effectiveness, although the Home Office claims that some 60 individuals departed and a further 65 were in the process of departing at the time of the evaluation. The project generated considerable comment in the popular press.

Remarkably, there has been little monitoring of this incremental expansion of reach. The NAO in 2020 stated that the Home Office was unable to assess whether the aim of increasing the number of immigrants choosing to leave the UK voluntarily had been achieved.

Those immigrants who are affected by the hostile environment, including the Windrush scandal, may be forced into homelessness or dependency on charity, engage in irregular work at risk of modern slavery and even too afraid to seek health and social care. Griffiths and Yeo (2021) outline key areas where the hostile environment has been found to be fundamentally flawed, giving rise to unintended consequences. These include the selectiveness of checking processes and inappropriate incentives for third parties responsible for monitoring.

Windrush

The outcome of the amalgam of various hostile environment measures is that access to government services and benefits is severely curtailed for those without immigration status or, importantly, without documentation establishing immigration status. This latter category came to the fore with the 'Windrush scandal', which saw Caribbean workers who had been brought to the UK between 1948 and 1971, and lived in the UK for decades without having to prove their status, being forced to leave. Others arrived in the UK as citizens with their rights protected by law and not physical documents. As Griffiths and Yeo (2021) observe, 'the fatal flaw … is the conflation of being undocumented and unlawfully resident'.

The scandal shone a spotlight on the hostile environment policies and Home Office administration of them. An independent report (Williams, 2020) observed that attempts to deter illegal migration in the 2010s, combined with outsourcing of immigration control to third parties and an insular culture in the Home Office that discounted warnings of adverse consequences, all contributed to the attempted deportation of Windrush immigrants escalating into a national scandal.

Slaven (2022) explores how the Windrush scandal became possible, arguing that British immigration governance underwent a shift towards scrutiny of individual qualification for continued residency rights that has created a lasting legacy in relation to postcolonial immigration, especially by allowing for the deracialisation of immigration policy.

Citizenship Revocation

The removal of citizenship is possible when an individual is considered to have been 'disloyal' to the state, a term which covers treason, terrorism and other acts considered to be a threat to national security. Citizenship can also be removed if an individual is considered to have obtained their citizenship fraudulently.

In a recent controversial case, Shamima Begum travelled to Syria at the age of 15 and married a member of the Islamic State. In 2019 the Home Secretary made an order to deprive Begum of her citizenship. Begum subsequently appealed, and in February 2021, the Supreme Court found that she did not have the right to re-enter the UK. This high-profile case received considerable media attention throughout 2021 and beyond. The case brought to public attention the fragility of citizenship and underscored the disquiet that came from the Windrush scandal.

Brexit

Political ruptures like Brexit not only have practical implications on foreigners living in the UK, but also create uncertainties and even danger. Brexit transformed some Europeans' sense of stable belonging into a state of limbo. Well-established French citizens in the UK felt ambiguities regarding their sense of belonging in the UK (Reed-Danahay, 2020)—as did migrants from the Nordic countries who also questioned their sense of social inclusion (2019, p. 172). The point is that although a sense of belonging often deepens and becomes stronger with time, political occurrences that challenge a person's legal status and rights might influence people's sense of belonging. Many of the large French diaspora said they felt 'betrayed and rejected by the UK' (Reed-Danahay, 2020, p. 23).

We find it apt to ask if this particular rupture also had an impact on how the French, and other migrants from EU member countries, regarded being taxed in the UK. Although taxation was only marginally impacted by Brexit, the four freedoms—free movement of goods, services, people and capital granted by the European Union—were. Indirectly income taxation was implicated; if you are not allowed to work, you cannot pay tax. As a Danish respondent told Koikkalainen:

> Brexiteers have told me to shut up and go home to my own country as the issue of Brexit is only to be discussed and decided by British people ... Ever since I came to the UK I have worked and paid taxes, but now I am not allowed an opinion about the future of the UK? (Koikkalainen, 2019, p. 178)

His entire contribution while working and paying tax in the UK is thus questioned by Brexit. For our participants the connection between tax and citizenship was more immediate and reconciled via the ability to work. Molly, born in Scandinavia, was just one of many of our participants who 'finally got her act together, swallowed the cost and applied for British citizenship' when Brexit created a wave of uncertainty among migrants.

Migrants in the Fiscal Field

All working migrants are required to pay income tax and national insurance contributions on the same basis as all other working UK residents. For income tax, formal citizenship status is not relevant. The criteria for establishing tax residence for income tax are based largely on duration of physical presence in the UK.

There are no specific income tax incentives for migrants, although the special rules applying to non-domiciled taxpayers can be considered an incentive. Domicile refers to the place deemed to be a permanent home over the course of a life, and persons with non-UK domicile may not have to pay tax on income earned outside of the UK until such time as it is remitted to the UK. Short-term migrants, who come to the UK for a limited time or do not spend much time in the UK, may not become tax resident, in which case foreign income and gains will not be taxed in the UK. A study by Advani and colleagues shows migrants are prevalent in the top of UK income distribution; indeed 85% of the rise in the top 1% share over the past two decades comes from migrants (Advani et al., 2025).

Migrants do not have full access to the welfare and benefits system, nor do they have free access to the NHS, until they have gained ILR status. For some, the fee for accessing NHS services is seen as a tax on migrants, understandably so, although in policy terms it is not counted as a 'tax'. Once migrants have gained ILR status, they may claim the full range of welfare benefits available in the UK and can freely use the NHS. There is a separate system for asylum seekers and refugees.

So how do migrants navigate the fiscal field? With difficulty it seems, but it is hard to know how much of the difficulties experienced are also experienced by native Brits, given the complexity of the UK tax and welfare systems. Those for whom English is a second language may struggle, but HMRC, as with other government departments, provides a considerable amount of translated information. But as noted by some of our participants, it is not just English language that is difficult, but also the technical jargon that is a feature of the fiscal field and acts as an exclusionary device for migrants and natives alike. The policy of self-regulation also creates difficulties, especially for those migrants who come from different fiscal cultures and may not be familiar with the need to register and file self-assessment tax returns for income tax. For those who are employed, without other sources of income, income tax and national insurance are dealt with by the employer, and most employees are happy to assume, rightly or wrongly, that this is done correctly. Interaction with HMRC in this scenario is minimal. For the self-employed and investor, interaction with HMRC is a necessary evil and most seek advice from professional advisers or from other sources of information, including social networks and social media (Onu & Oats, 2016).

The Low Incomes Tax Reform Group (LITRG) provides help for non-English speakers to navigate the tax system. The organisation, an initiative of the Chartered Institute of Taxation, provides guidance and videos, translated into different languages, to help migrants understand where to get tax help. Often this will entail referral to a tax adviser.

Certainly, migrants are vulnerable to exploitation by unscrupulous advisers and our evidence is that they find direct interaction with HMRC difficult. Our participants are all well-educated professionals, and yet most of them recounted tales of problematic relations with HMRC.

Reflections

Fiscal policy in the UK is an important area of public policy that is largely developed in the political field and implemented in the bureaucratic field. The UK fiscal field comprises two activities, taxing and spending, that are not always considered together. For decades now, notwithstanding the ideological differences between left and right governments, the prevailing ethos in UK public policy has included individualism, self-regulation, short termism and marketisation. There is also uncritical acceptance of largely positivist scholarly expertise, which is different from other (assumed to be softer) forms of knowledge generated, for example, in the social sciences beyond economics and law. The combination of individualism and positivist expertise is most clearly seen in the enthusiastic adoption of behavioural insights (nudge) techniques in a number of public policy fields including both the fiscal and immigration fields.

Although the fiscal field incorporates the spending side as well as the taxing side, our study primarily focuses on tax. Here we find public policy developed within a narrow selection of technical experts with little input from the wider populace or the scholarly field. The Treasury is dominant in developing tax policy and constraining the actions of politicians in relation to tax changes, whereas the practical aspects of maintaining the policy in action is dominated by HMRC. The organisational culture of the Treasury and HMRC privileges economic and tax technical knowledge respectively, and as autonomous organisations they are largely resistant to political or other external intervention. The academic voice is particularly muted in the UK fiscal field, especially in relation to tax policy.

Our fieldwork consists of talking about tax with well-educated migrants to the UK who carry some and in some cases extensive knowledge of the taxes. We aimed to explore their views and relationship to tax, both in their domestic and in their adopted country, the UK. For migrants to the UK, travelling through the fiscal field can be stressful and frustrating, even with the passage of time.

References

Advani, A. 2022. Who does and doesn't pay taxes? *Fiscal Studies* 43 (1): 5–22.

Advani, A., F. Koenig, L. Pessina, and A. Summers. 2025. Immigration and the top 1 percent. *The Review of Economics and Statistics* 107 (4): 1123–1135.

Bourdieu, P., and L. J. D. Wacquant. 1992. *An invitation to reflexive sociology*. University of Chicago Press.

Brooks, R. 2013. *The great tax robbery: How Britain became a tax haven for fat cats and big business*. Oneworld Publications.

Brooks, T. 2019. The life in the UK citizenship test and the urgent need for its reform. In *Citizenship in times of turmoil? Theory, practice and policy*, ed. D. Prabhat, 22–60. Edward Elgar.

Byrne, B. 2019. Naturalisation and becoming a citizen in the UK. In *Citizenship in times of turmoil? Theory, practice and policy*, ed. D. Prabhat, 61–78. Edward Elgar.

Clery, E. (2023). *A liberalisation in attitudes?* National Centre for Social Research, British Social Attitudes Report 40.

Closs-Davies, S., K. P. R. Bartels, and D. M. Merkl-Davies. 2020. The frog in the pan: Relational transformation of public values in the UK tax authority. *Accounting, Auditing and Accountability Journal* 34 (7): 1635–1663.

De Widt, D., and L. Oats. 2024. Imagining cooperative tax regulation: Common origins, divergent paths. *Critical Perspectives on Accounting* 99 (2024): 102446.

Demenge, V., and M. Robert. 2024. Public the bureaucratic field and the sociology of public policy: From the structure of the administration to the production of policies. In *Bringing Bourdieu's theory of fields to critical policy analysis*, ed. V. Dubois, 109–127. Edward Elgar.

DiMaggio, P. J., and W. W. Powell. 1983. The iron cage revisited: Institutional isomorphism and collective rationality in organizational fields. *American Sociological Review* 48 (2): 147–160.

Eshan, R. (2023). *Our society: Integrating Britain's communities* (Independent Report). https://rakibehsan.com/our-society-integrating-britains-communities/

Fligstein, N., and D. McAdam. 2012. *A theory of fields*. Oxford: Oxford University Press.
Goodfellow, M. 2019. *Hostile environment: How immigrants became scapegoats*. Verso.
Gracia, L., and L. Oats. 2012. Boundary work and tax regulation: A Bourdieusian view. *Accounting Organizations and Society* 37 (5): 304–321.
Griffiths, M., and C. Yeo. 2021. The UK'S hostile environment: Deputising immigration control. *Critical Social Policy* 41 (4): 521–544.
Harvey, M. 2019. Discrimination in British nationality law. In *Citizenship in times of turmoil? Theory, practice and policy*, ed. D. Prabhat, 2–21. Edward Elgar.
Hastings, A., and P. Matthews. 2015. Bourdieu and the big society: Empowering the powerful in public service provision? *Policy and Politics* 43 (4): 545–560.
Hillman, N. 2014. *In defence of special advisers: Lessons from personal experience*. Institute for Government.
Kauppi, N. 2018. Transnational social fields. In *The Oxford handbook of Pierre Bourdieu*, ed. T. Medvetz and J. J. Sallaz, 183–199. Oxford University Press. https://doi.org/10.1093/oxfordhb/9780199357192.013.8
Keep, M. (2023). *Taxation statistics* (House of Commons Briefing Paper No. CBP 8513).
Knox, T., and D. Lilley. 2023. *An analysis of the effect of taxes and benefits on household income*. Civitas: Institute for the Study of Civil Society.
Koikkalainen, S. 2019. Nordic ties and British lives? Migrant capital and the case of Nordic migrants living in London. *Social Inclusion* 7 (4): 171–180.
Lewin, K. 1951. *Field theory in social science*. Harper & Brothers.
Martin, J. L. 2003. What is field theory? *The American Journal of Sociology* 109 (1): 1–49.
NAO (National Audit Office). (2020). *The management of tax expenditures* (Report HC48, House of Commons Session 2019–2020). https://www.nao.org.uk/reports/the-management-of-tax-expenditures/?nab=2
O'Grady, T. 2022. *Transformation of British welfare policy*. Oxford University Press.
van Oers, R. 2014. *Deserving citizenship: Citizenship tests in Germany, The Netherlands and the United Kingdom*. Martinus Nijhoff.
Onu, D., and L. Oats. 2016. Paying tax is part of life: Social norms and social influence in tax communications. *Journal of Economic Behavior and Organization* 124:29–42.
Prabhat, D. 2018. *Britishness, belonging and citizenship*. Bristol University Press/Polity.
Prabhat, D. 2019. Introduction. In *Citizenship in times of turmoil? Theory, practice and policy*, ed. D. Prabhat, xi–xvii. Edward Elgar.
Reed-Danahay, D. 2020. Brexit, liminality, and ambiguities of belonging. French citizens in London. *Ethnologia Europaea* 50 (2): 16–31.

Rose, R. 1987. Steering the ship of state: One tiller but two pairs of hands. *British Journal of Political Science* 17 (4): 409–433. https://doi.org/10.1017/S0007123400004853.
Slaven, M. 2022. The Windrush scandal and the individualization of postcolonial immigration control in Britain. *Ethnic and Racial Studies* 45 (16): 49–71.
Stanley, L. 2018. "When we were just giving stuff away willy-nilly": Historicizing contemporary British tax morale. In *The leap of faith. The fiscal foundations of successful government in Europe and America*, ed. S. Steinmo and J. D'Attoma, 155–177. Oxford University Press.
Thomas, A., R. Clyne, M. Bishop, and A. Lilly. 2022. *A new statutory role for the civil service*. Institute for Government.
Tuck, P. 2013. The changing role of tax governance: Remaking the large corporate taxpayer into a visible customer partner. *British Journal of Management* 24 (S3): 116–131. https://doi.org/10.1111/1467-8551.12031.
Tuck, P., D. de Cogan, and J. Snape. 2019. A tale of the merger between the inland revenue and HM customs and excise. In *Studies in the history of tax law*, ed. P. Harris and D. de Cogan, vol. 9, 213–241. Bloomsbury Publishing.
Wacquant, L. 2015. Crafting the neoliberal state: Workfare and prisonfare in the bureaucratic field. In *Bourdieu's theory of social fields: Concepts and applications*, ed. M. Hilgers and E. Mangez, 238–256. Routledge.
Williams, W. 2020. *Windrush lessons learned review*. The Home Office.

CHAPTER 4

Facets of Fiscal Belonging

Abstract The focus here is migrants' views on taxes. Fiscal citizenship as a concept was difficult to relate to for migrants that have arrived in a country for manifold reasons—for work, fleeing war, staying on after completing an education, for love, etc. Although many migrants may have contributed to their adopted society by paying taxes for a long, long time, some have not achieved formal citizenship. We thus see a need to expand our understanding of citizenship beyond the formal/legal domain to better draw on the stories of migrants. Inspired by Nira Yuval-Davis' facets of belonging, we propose four facets of fiscal belonging: work, family, (social) acceptance and (political and cultural) values. This allows us to show how the notion of belonging is articulated in relation to tax and citizenship.

Keywords Belonging • Work • Family • Acceptance • Values

Facets of Fiscal Belonging

Our participants did talk differently about taxation. As a start, we take a step backwards and look at a few definitions of fiscality—as all matters concerning taxation.

Definitions of tax are multiple and often political. They follow the numerous academic disciplines that take an interest in tax, as we saw in Chap. 1, but also vary in the supposedly apolitical encyclopaedias.

L. Björklund Larsen, L. Oats, *Crossing Borders, Sharing Burdens*,
https://doi.org/10.1007/978-3-031-99394-7_4

Many encyclopaedias take the old-fashioned view that taxation is extractive and a forced contribution (Levi, 1988). A similar definition is offered by the Swedish National encyclopaedia: 'Tax is a statutory payment to the public without direct reciprocity' (Nationalencyklopedin). Encyclopaedia Britannica follows suit proposing that taxation is the 'imposition of compulsory levies on individuals or entities by governments', but continues and takes a more encompassing view citing American economist Richard A. Musgrave: 'the purpose of taxation … is to distinguish between objectives of resource allocation, income redistribution, and economic stability' (Encyclopaedia Britannica). Leftist political ideologies embrace taxes, whereas conservatives on the right value individuals' economic freedom to decide, often advocating for less tax.

Similarly, how the taxpayer regards taxes has implications for how fiscal belonging is defined. Seeing taxes as something taken from you is obviously very different from seeing taxes as your contribution to society and community or as a reciprocal act where you now, or in the future, will be cared for by public welfare expenditure. Our point here is not to point the finger in one or other definition; it is just to note that how people regard taxes in relation to belonging also depends on their view about taxes generally.

Nira Yuval-Davis' three facets of belonging is the starting point for our analysis of how migrants relate to paying tax and belonging (we provided a description of her theory in Chap. 2). It is worth repeating that the different facets are interrelated but separate from each other (Yuval-Davis, 2011, p. 8) which clearly resonates with our findings. We also use facets as we agree with her that levels would make for hierarchies; this is not relevant when people reason around tax and sense of belonging. Importantly, our participants almost unanimously reflected on a society in motion with the result that their views and understanding of their place in society is subject to continuous change. It is against this background our participants create a sense of belonging through talking about tax.

To repeat in her words: 'The first facet concerns social locations, the second relates to people's identifications and emotional attachments to various collectivities and groupings; and the third relates to ethical and political value systems with which people judge their own and others' belonging. These different facets are interrelated but cannot be reduced to each other' (Yuval-Davis, 2011, p. 8). Yuval-Davis' facets have inspired our analysis, but we think a bit differently.

Introducing fiscal belonging leads us to look slightly differently at taxation. We propose four facets: *work, family, acceptance* and *values*. Our facets are more actor driven than those suggested by Yuval-Davies as we interpret how people talk about being taxed in relation to feeling at home, as belonging. In addition to the four facets, we recognise the importance of reciprocity which underlies and overlays fiscal belonging and which we conceive of as being thin or thick. Reciprocity is an issue that reinforces but can also weaken the facets, and we come back to this in Chap. 5.

Work is for most migrants the very basis for surviving and for many a first place where feelings of attachment are formed. An employee qua immigrant acquires a boss and colleagues, people who are usually natives. Work is a fundamental way of belonging in a new country and establishing and shaping relations beyond the immediate family (and friends). Getting a job is also for most the very start of recognising paying tax, like the natives do. Although there is value added tax (VAT), it is usually not paid attention to in everyday life. It is baked into the formal price, and there is no way to get away from paying VAT unless you engage in buying products or services informally (e.g. without a receipt). We find that the type of employment offered through work is an important dimension of this facet. The self-employed do not necessarily have colleagues, but instead customers and competitors, but through longer-term commitments and relations with clients, a similar sense of belonging is established.

Family, including being married to a native, can lead to an increased sense of belonging. The stay then becomes more long term, there is a longevity in being more attached to the new country and thinking about life beyond the next couple of years. Having children increases such a feeling. They get healthcare, go to schools and get educated, acquire friends and develop their own interests and take part in all sorts of activities. But family relations can also weaken the sense of belonging to a new place. If it is within the (extended) family that most of the relational activities take place, it might be easy to retain the 'old' ways of being and/or seeing the world (Fischer, 2017).

Acceptance is an internal, almost emotional feeling. This facet comes quite close to Yuval-Davis' second facet: the one around people's identification and emotional attachment. Ours relates to the feeling and perception that people around you recognise you, acknowledge you and even adapt to you. Being accepted is feeling at home through friendships, of finding pastimes and activities where interaction with natives becomes natural—being naturally included in society whether it is being greeted by neighbours or the local baker, or engaged in local activities on the same conditions as anybody else. It is not forced upon you, but rather felt in various ways. A strong feeling of acceptance strengthens the ability to contribute with taxes in the same way as do those—community, society—you feel accepted by. You belong more to the community that accepts you than to the tax collecting entity.

With *values* we include both political and cultural values. It concerns sharing values held by the society in which you reside. We are generalising here; the values are not necessarily all values existing in a society, but those that substantially make up and define understanding the adopted, the new country. It is about agreeing to the political but also administrative system of the country. This can include how taxation is conducted, and how the national tax administration operates and communicates with its taxpayers. From a critical social science perspective, taxation has a redistributive element and is also reciprocal. Taxes and the act of collecting and spending tax ought to be a large ingredient in our understanding of how people relate to the community and society that they feel they belong to. So, there are really two questions. When you pay tax, do you feel you belong to a given society? And when you feel like you belong, you more willingly pay taxes?

The collector certainly engages in strategies to enhance feelings of belonging. Marcelo Bergman and Sven Steinmo argue that there are several state actions where the aim has been to create a sense of belonging in order to make people more willing to comply with taxes (2018, p. 277). Such actions make states and society seem to have a common purpose. That tax money belongs to the people can be articulated in many different ways. The Swedish social democrats, that ruled Sweden for forty years and built most of the welfare infrastructure, stated in the late 1950s that 'tax belonged to everyone' (Jansson, 2018, p. 65), whereas the Catholic Church in Italy encouraged citizens to avoid state taxes and instead pay to institutions—the church—so that taxes were redistributed in a fair way. It was argued that taxes belonged to the Italian people but the way they were redistributed in Italy served only its administrative and political elites (Hien, 2018, p. 94).

Could it even be, as Tsilly Dagan argues, that the ease by which current migration takes place is altering the interaction between states and their constituents? Does the combination of taxpayers' mobility and many states seeming to offer a possibility to 'consume public goods and services à-la-carte' (Dagan, 2022) threaten to transform taxpayers from equal members of a political community into consumers of public goods and services? Such a person is transformed from a responsible taxpayer/citizen into a shopper for public services, but one that does not necessarily contribute to the public good/s. This perhaps aligns with tax administration's change in vocabulary, from taxpayer to customer (e.g. Björklund Larsen, 2024, p. 180; Tuck, 2013).

Work

Having the right to work, a job, proper employment, a business, makes for belonging. At work, one learns the ropes from colleagues. Work not only creates financial security, but it also provides access to insurance and other societal institutions as well as to colleagues. Tax on income from work was the first and foremost fiscal issue our participants addressed—unanimously. Paying income tax provides a distinct and important direct connection to the state. Our participants were well educated and thus have income above the threshold for paying income tax. For them, as for most UK taxpayers with income above a certain level, work is the main source of paying tax. They work, they contribute—which they feel morally obliged to do—and this contribution also creates expectations on society. It makes for an increased sense of belonging.

The income tax threshold also poses a problem. Many migrants, although 'gainfully employed' as Colleen who comes from the Caribbean, puts it, might not pay income tax as they do not earn enough. She sees this as problematic as they might not be able to feel that they contribute. It might therefore be easier for them to justify doing additional work that is conducted under the radar from His Majesty's Revenue and Customs (HMRC)—and thus not taxed.

Gertrud, born and educated in Scandinavia, thinks a lot about the other end of the income spectrum—the high earners in society. She sees them as usually happily understanding and accepting the need to contribute with taxes; they can afford it and also understand what taxes are for. The ultra-rich might be a different matter. Many of our participants voiced the opinion that they somehow float above the average Brit and therefore try to avoid paying as much as possible. They appear to not belong to Britain or feel British but belong to a class of their own (cf. Barbulescu, 2018). One can speculate about the feeling of belonging for those who moved to Britain due to taxes being lower than in their home country. Is the comparison of tax rates between places a creator of belonging? Or do these often very wealthy people belong anywhere and nowhere?[1]

Where and how wealth among native Brits has been amassed is another source of resistance for George to feel like he belongs. He is the great-great-grandson of enslaved Africans whose middle name he bears, and he argues that much of the old wealth in Britain derives from plantations in the Caribbean, old wealth that his great-great-grandfather toiled to build. As he said with emphasis, 'So would it be amiss if some of my Caribbean brothers and sisters were having a problem paying taxes in the UK, you know?'

Not only are race, economic history and colonialism important when talking about belonging, but added to this is the fact of being self-employed. George runs several businesses and is thus also self-employed. He has no problem communicating with the tax authority, HMRC, he says, and claims to be fine with the taxes he has to pay. What he objects to is what is lacking at the policy level as 'there are structures and loopholes by which people can escape paying taxes. I think it would be silly to expect that someone would pay what they don't have to pay'. He also advocates for a wealth tax as he compares his own situation as a newcomer with established Brits who might have inherited a house and are able to pass on 'tremendously more wealth to their children than I arguably could'. The facets of belonging to the social category of self-employed and Caribbean, the emotional identification with slave ancestry and living in an unequal society which merits old and new wealth make for a powerful cocktail in George's account.

Talking about tax is rare for those who are in employment. Operation of the employer income tax withholding system (PAYE) system means they seldom think about taxes. Although Rosie is employed, she is still stressed when thinking about tax. She ran her own business for a while but got really stressed thinking that she could have made a mistake when reporting to HMRC. That was the main reason for her finding employment. It is not just about the profession but how various types of employment demand different tax reporting and payment. How income taxes are constructed regarding types of employment makes for different types of belonging. Formerly self-employed Rosie finds paying tax more relaxed when the PAYE system takes care of her contribution.

[1] None of our participants had moved to Britain because tax rates were lower. The reasons were otherwise and often in combination: work, studies, love and political.

Work, then, is an important facet in fiscal belonging and serves both social and economic roles. It provides colleagues to learn from and an income to survive on, but also financial ties to the state. Minimum thresholds for paying tax on work undermine this connection and so do historical recollections of who has contributed to the wealth of society. The ultra-rich are seen to adopt a similar connection to the state but at the other end of the income spectrum. Descendants from slaves recollect that their ancestors toiled for nothing while bringing wealth to the British emporium, whereas some believe that today's ultra-rich contribute so much just being rich, and thus big spenders and possibly providing employment opportunities, that they do not need to pay tax.

Family

Having children can enhance a sense of belonging. Migrants see a future for their children in their new country and want to invest in their chances of a good life.

Jake sees home both in the UK and in South Africa. He has spent equal amounts of time in both countries but chose for political reasons to leave South Africa. He belongs firmly to the UK, despite having parents and other relatives left in South Africa. Belonging is a way to look to the future as he and his immediate family lives and will continue to live in the UK.

Molly is strongly attached to the UK. 'All my friendships and my children and my family are here. So my day-to-day life is here. This is home in my day-to-day life'. She sees voting for what taxes will be used for as important, arguing it is because her children live here. 'You have to know that your children *and* your grandparents are cared for'. Family makes for a longer-term perspective on being part of and belonging to a society.

Although Alison is married to a Brit, she never had children in the UK. She talks about belonging to the UK *for the moment*, but it's not a black and white feeling. Her longer commitment to her adopted country seems mostly personal, thinking about her retirement but not beyond that. This differs from both Molly and Jake whose children are growing up and studying in the UK.

Colin, on the other hand, feels at home in Southern Europe, the country where he was born. It is a sentimental attachment but also something he keeps active by travelling back very often, both for work-related reasons and for vacation. He has travelled so much that he does not feel very engaged in British society. He is married to a woman from his native country; they eat native food at home and he speaks his mother tongue with his wife but not so much with his kids. It is mainly through the activities of his kids that he feels a sense of belonging to the UK. People's views on taxes to his mind do not depend on people's migration status. People just have different views and those derive from upbringing but also on how you are treated and if you perceive the tax system as fair and transparent.

Family is important for creating a sense of belonging. Having children makes for an especially strong attachment: they go to school; they create friendships; they participate in social activities like sports, scouts and cultural activities; they will most probably build a future in the country. Family makes you not only see the immediate concerns of your relation to the state but also provide a longer perspective.

Social Acceptance

Many of our respondents spoke about friendships and other relations that had developed over time in their adopted country, creating a stronger sense of belonging. Paulina, coming from South America, belongs in Britain. 'I feel much more, much more comfortable living here, not only in the UK, but in London, in my little pocket of "a good neighbourhood"[2] because I made friendships, really strong friendships'. (We will get to know Paulina more in Chap. 6.)

Belonging for Anne is not so much about the place itself but mainly about the people—where her family and friends are. She misses the culture, the kindness and the humour back home but has to a certain extent found it in London, especially with compatriots and other foreigners. Anne talks about belonging as being accepted in various social spaces: with her friends, at work, but also in the activities she pursues outside work—her pastimes and her passions. She was brought up with 'paying tax', and she says that she is now in a decent position to contribute, so taxes are not something she gets too upset about. Paying up is just part of everyday life.

For the two black men from the Caribbean, especially, there were clear references to not fitting in because of race. They talked about looking different from most (white) British males and also about moving and body posture in other ways. Their sense of belonging was also weakened due to what they perceived as biased politics towards black people. They talked about not being accepted for what they look like. Peter proves an

[2] The actual name of the London suburb has been anonymised in order to protect Paulina's identity.

illustrative example. He was born in the Caribbean but has lived in the Birmingham area since the 1960s. His parents are British; he is a British resident and has worked all his life as a legal counsellor. Yet, experiences of discrimination have made it difficult for him to see Britain as home. He belongs elsewhere—where people look and behave like he does. For those born in the Caribbean, belonging meant a clear nostalgia for emotional and cultural attachment to the islands. As Peter said, 'if I go a day and don't read the local paper [from my native island], my day is miserable. I have to read it, I need to know what is going on', and this is despite not having any family left there and not being back since 2008. Belonging is for Peter 'the sense of being among people who look like you, share a similar history and having family "in the island"'. Although Peter's children live in the UK, as does his sister and her family, he does not see it as home. His home is a search for roots: Peter even spoke about Africa and in particular Ghana as home, as his ancestors came from there.

George was also born and raised in the Caribbean and came to England as an adult and spoke of lack of networks. In his view, this comes naturally to native Brits through upbringing and education, but there is also a racial content involved in lacking networks. Despite the UK having immigrants from all over the world, he still feels that being black makes him stand out in Britain; not looking like the majority excludes him from networks and is thus an impediment to truly belonging in Britain. Compare his experience with that of Jake, a 'white' South African, who left his native country because he and his wife were not 'happy politically' there (see also the next section). Although Jake thinks of himself as South African, has family there and loves South Africa, he would never want to go and live there. He says he belongs in the UK. Jake has never doubted his belonging to the UK, and although a high earner, he happily pays tax here. George and Peter feel somewhat alienated due to their skin colour, and their willingness to comply with taxation is not as clear-cut. That willingness to evade and avoid taxes increases with level of income is thus complicated by the sense of fitting in physically.

There is also the risk that feelings of belonging wane when someone feels they belong in different countries. You do not know the past in your new society, whereas you increasingly lose track of what is happening in the place you migrated from. It begs the question of whether belonging can be weakened and you feel increasingly alienated.

Feeling and being accepted is important in life. It also seems important for the willingness to pay tax. If the majority of those with whom a taxpayer share their taxes regard them with suspicion, willingness to contribute seems to decline.

Sharing (Cultural/Political) Values

Within the term values we include both political and cultural values. This concerns sharing the values held by the society in which you reside. We are generalising here, not necessarily all values but those that substantially define a society. For example, two well-educated South Africans spoke about having left their country due to not being happy about the political situation there. Gary says: 'My value system is much more closely aligned with the UK in terms of my underlying philosophies and values around freedoms and around my cultural background related to South Africa. But I don't have a strong nationalistic feeling either way'. The same goes for Jake who left South Africa because he was not 'happy politically'. Jake reflected on his friends in South Africa. He thinks they are less happy to pay tax than he is, as their payments are not put to good use. There is much corruption, and public money that should go to advance society disappears, ending up in someone's private account. Gary and Jake have earned substantial amounts of money working in the UK finance sector, but Jake has now retired and Gary has moved on to another career path with substantially less income. Both have paid much in tax, but they say that they have never had any issues with it; if they referred to their income, they said it was rather an embarrassment to earn as much as they previously did.

Andrew, coming to Britain as a young refugee from the war-torn Balkans, thinks of himself as 'being a proud Brit'. Calling the UK home stems from moving at a moment in life when he started to shape his character. It was at the right moment when he left his country of birth for a secure and good place. Gary is more forthright in this regard: 'So it's as you know, it's about the functioning of a society'. Or as Colleen says, 'I see tax as really people pooling their resources together, so that whoever is handling what I would call things at the macro-level that they have some resources, that they can provide some facilities that can benefit us'. She likes her neighbourhood and willingly pays tax. 'I like the bus service. I like the fact that the place is clean. I like the fact that I feel safe when I'm getting home, no matter how late it is. And I know it's because of the tax that I am paying, so I don't have a problem with it'. Many people dislike the local government property tax (council tax) that is mainly used to fund local services because it is progressive, related to the value of your property, not how much it costs to have bins collected. Many have commented on its increase in recent times.

In contrast to our two male Caribbean participants, Molly, a white woman born in Scandinavia, recognises that her whiteness makes her more comfortable in the UK. But that is not the only reason. When she returns to her native country, there are always new institutions to relate to and understand. Those experiences 'make me feel less at home because I'm not confident of my knowledge of how to function very well'. She does not know how to navigate the new institutions and thus for each visit it strengthens her feelings towards Britain. Alison, originally from the same region, resonates with the opposite view. She says she does not understand the current (British) tax system. She thinks that the transparency, the predictability and the all-inclusiveness in the system in her native country is better than what for her is an incomprehensible and a one-to-one relationship with HMRC where tax rates almost seem negotiable. Not understanding the values behind the system makes you long for the system you left behind. If there are certain values you hold that are not prominent, or even pronounced in the new country's tax system, these values might be strengthened. In her view, there is an opacity in the UK system that restricts citizens from understanding how society is built; it is therefore difficult to understand what the state/government provides.

Reflections

This chapter has explored four facets of fiscal belonging. *Work* makes for an important facet in fiscal belonging. Migrants learn both professional skills, but especially the social culture existing in workplaces. It is in workplaces that views especially on income taxes are formed. Native workfellows provide colleagues to learn from and work provides an income and other financial ties to the state. Minimum thresholds for paying tax on work undermine this connection and so do historical recollections of who has contributed to the wealth of society. *Family* makes for longer-term commitment. It makes for thinking beyond oneself, thinking about a future for partners and children in their new country. Migrants feel the need to invest in infrastructure, education, good public services, etc. in order to increase children's possibilities of a good life as they grow up and build a future in the country. *Social acceptance* is a forceful ingredient. Feeling and being accepted just as one is—by looks and behaviour—is important in life. Ease of finding friends and acquaintances also seems important for willingness to pay tax. Among our participants was the inclination to share more of their taxes if people would not regard you with suspicion, if you look like the majority. Finally, sharing *values*, both cultural and political, makes for a stronger sense of belonging. This is seldom expressed at an individual level, but in a concoction of political debates, government policies in practice, media reporting—values that steer how society works. They do not necessarily need to be ideological, but come close to it.

We thus see in the observations of our participants a complex picture with many factors and influences that are difficult to disentangle. While our fieldwork revolves around the UK, we see glimpses of issues that resonate across different countries. Belonging, as we have shown, is a form of attachment to aspects of the society in which we live. Our interest is in fiscal belonging, which leads to the question of what does 'fiscal' entail. While volumes have been written on tax, and even more on welfare, little work brings these two aspects of the state's finances together. Yet the people we speak to, and popular discourse, does not separate these. This is most clearly seen in the context of reciprocity, which we come back to in Chap. 5.

References

Barbulescu, R. 2018. Global mobility corridors for the ultra-rich. The neoliberal transformation of citizenship. *IMISCOE Research Series* 81 (1): 29–32. https://doi.org/10.1007/978-3-319-92719-0_6.

Bergman, M., and S. H. Steinmo. 2018. Taxation and consent: Implications for developing nations. In *The leap of faith. The fiscal foundations of successful government in Europe and America*, ed. S. Steinmo, 273–292. Oxford University Press.

Björklund Larsen, L. 2024. Mottos for a more tax-compliant society: Strategies, tax compliance research, and fiscal practices at the Swedish tax agency. In *Anthropology and tax. Ethnographies of fiscal relations*, ed. J. Mugler, M. Sheild Johansson, and R. Smith, 178–199. Cambridge University Press.

Dagan, T. (2022). Klaus Vogel lecture 2021: Unbundled tax sovereignty—Refining the challenges. *Bulletin for International Taxation for International Taxation,* July, 318–328.

Encyclopaedia Britannica. (n.d.). *Britannica*. https://www.britannica.com. Retrieved December 2, 2024.

Fischer, C. 2017. Imagined communities? Relations of social identities and social organisation among Afghan diaspora groups in Germany and the UK. *Journal of Intercultural Studies* 38 (1): 18–35. https://doi.org/10.1080/07256868.2016.1269060.

Hien, J. 2018. Tax evasion in Italy: A god-given right? In *The leap of faith. The fiscal foundations of successful government in Europe and America*, ed. S. Steinmo, 81–105. Oxford University Press.

Jansson, J. 2018. Creating tax-compliant citizens in Sweden. The role of social democracy. In *The leap of faith. The fiscal foundations of successful government in Europe and America*, ed. S. Steinmo, 56–80. Oxford University Press.

Levi, M. 1988. *Of rule and revenue*. University of California Press.

Nationalencyklopedin (Swedish National Encyclopedia). (n.d.). *Nationalencyklopedin*. Retrieved December 1, 2023, from https://www.ne.se/

Tuck, P. 2013. The changing role of tax governance: Remaking the large corporate taxpayer into a visible customer partner. *British Journal of Management* 24 (S3): 116–131. https://doi.org/10.1111/1467-8551.12031.

Yuval-Davis, N. 2011. *The politics of belonging: Intersectional contestations*. SAGE.

CHAPTER 5

Reciprocity Thick and Thin

Abstract We explore how the concept of reciprocity enriches our understanding of taxation beyond its traditional definition as a compulsory, unrequited payment. This chapter aims to take seriously the many sentiments people express that in essence mean 'getting something for your money'. Yet, as we will show, there is seldom a simple tit-for-tat reasoning underlying this sentiment. Instead, we introduce *thin* and *thick* reciprocity to be able to nuance, but also bringing more depth and flesh, to the four facets of fiscal belonging. While what we refer to as thin reciprocity may dominate policy models and compliance research due to its measurability, we argue that thick reciprocity, which is harder to quantify, provides essential insights into civic solidarity, identity and moral engagement with the state.

Keywords Varieties of reciprocity • Tax compliance • Thin reciprocity • Thick reciprocity

Talking about tax, our participants had many reflections on 'getting something for your money'. It regards acknowledging receipt of reciprocal services and welfare but is also about investment in the future. Broadly, it is a give and take view on taxes in relation to public authorities but also to other citizens. As critical tax scholars we are trying to understand how people perceive paying tax. Throughout our research with various

L. Björklund Larsen, L. Oats, *Crossing Borders, Sharing Burdens*,
https://doi.org/10.1007/978-3-031-99394-7_5

stakeholders in the tax arena, we heard arguments that taxes are paid in order to accomplish something—to get something back. This is far from the common definition of tax, e.g. 'a compulsory, unrequited payment to general government' (Keen & Slemrod, 2021, p. 3) or 'imposition of compulsory levies on individuals or entities by governments' (Encyclopaedia Britannica).

Erich Kirchler calls our attention to the many different sentiments that taxation engenders among taxpayers—and also points out that taxes create expectations:

> It has been argued that most people recognize the need for contributing to the public budget and are aware of public goods, nevertheless their feelings towards taxes are most frequently negative. Taxes are either perceived as a loss of personal freedom to decide about investment of one's own money, as contributions without a fair return, or as a repeated request by the government to plug the gaps in the state's finances which are caused by inefficient management of politicians. (1998, p. 120)

People's willingness to pay tax increases when they expect to get something in return or they pay for benefits received (cf. Leroy, 2008). Such reciprocity is a powerful justification for paying tax and the literature is replete with different aspects of how it plays a role in our willingness to pay tax. As reciprocity is defined in different ways (Björklund Larsen, 2018; cf. Gribnau, 2015), we find a need to rethink how we see reciprocity. This will lead to two types of reciprocity that provide a more dynamic dimension to our facets of belonging.

Reciprocity comes from Latin via French, *reciprocitè*. There are many definitions, but overall it refers to the status of a relation or an action between people, countries or organisations that is governed by a mutual exchange of commercial or other privileges. It can thus be both a status and an action and can denote various types of exchanges. No wonder the concept has found a multitude of usages.

Taxation has been researched by many disciplines, as has reciprocity. It is noteworthy how the concept of reciprocity within taxation has received different meanings across disciplines. What follows is an overview of how reciprocity has been used in tax research in order to arrive at how we inductively apply the concept.

Reciprocity and Tax

Reciprocal behaviour is always posed as a response to those of other actors—perceived, real, imagined. Reciprocity is a disposition to cooperate with others, but also to punish those who cooperate for reasons of self-interest; it is a norm that makes people comply with tax rules. 'Acting under this norm an individual will respond to another's act in the same way in which that person treated him' (Kornhauser, 2007, p. 9). If a person is treated with generosity and kindness, they will respond in kind, whereas if treated badly the response will be in the same fashion. The implication of a strong norm of reciprocity is also said to apply to taxes: if others are perceived to pay so will I, whereas if no one else complies why would I (ibid., p. 7; Slemrod, 1992)? Reciprocity thus needs careful nurturing as its impact on tax compliance can go both ways.

For legal scholars, the notion of reciprocity is approached in terms of relationships between legal subjects. Legal scholars, for example, propose that a reciprocal relation between an omni-powerful tax administration and an individual taxpayer makes for a legal (asymmetric) relationship between taxpayer and tax administration (Gribnau, 2015), most noteworthy in how they communicate. Reciprocity also exists between the law-giver and taxpayers (Gribnau, 2013). The starting point from a legal perspective is that a relation can be balanced neither between state and individual nor between different taxpayers. They have different resources and may not be equal before the law. Discussing reciprocity in this way draws on philosophical notions in order to achieve a more equal status in the tax arena where counterparties are seen as unequal by definition. Inequality has implications; the reciprocal relation between in essence two unequal parties means that a fair exchange has to be carefully maintained (Westerman, 2014). Seeing reciprocity in this way provides a power dimension to taxation—that not all taxpayers are treated equally. Reciprocity cannot be presupposed and is not a given, and it follows that the law itself should be presupposed to facilitate reciprocity as a desirable feature. There is therefore a continuous need for legal and political intervention to secure a fair and equitable relation between citizens but also between tax authorities and citizens (ibid., p. 184).

A tax authority is the right hand of the state and has considerable powers to collect revenue and investigate taxpayers' (economic) lives. If a tax administration needs to enforce compliance through reciprocal norms it has to communicate on an equal footing so that taxpayers may understand

and respect the intention of the law. Taxpayers should not fear the law but respect it for the benefit of societal good. Because of the complexity of tax law, tax administrations can seldom explain this in a reciprocal, communicative way. This can give rise to unintentional non-compliance—and even over-compliance—resulting in a violation of legal certainty and equality (Gribnau, 2015, pp. 205–206). Is it appropriate to ask, as does Hans Gribnau, what are the implications for tax compliance if the communication of tax law is governed by the principle of reciprocity as opposed to law as top-down command (Gribnau, 2015)?

In our inductive research of migrants' views on taxes, the power dimension was not referred to as much as the feeling of receiving something in return.

This type of reasoning is also explored by economists and political scientists. They have, for example, tested taxpayers' willingness to comply applying theories of pro-social behaviour, where the argument is that people are more inclined to do what others do. In this vein of tax compliance research, reciprocity means that if other taxpayers pay their due taxes, other citizens would also feel obliged to pay. And the opposite also applies; in a context where many avoid paying tax, the propensity for the individual taxpayer to do the same is greater (Rabin, 1998; Fehr & Falk, 2002).

Reciprocity is said to be one of the explanatory norms in research on tax compliance and evasion (Alm, 2012); he even proposes that the concept will be one of five research directions governing future research on tax evasion. James Alm acknowledges the many insights made over the last 40 years, yet also articulates many outstanding issues that are yet to be investigated, dug into more deeply or explored. Thus economics is not the only source of theoretical explanation.

In social behavioural/psychological models, reciprocity in relation to tax compliance is dichotomised in various ways; as either strong–weak, negative–positive or horizontal–vertical. Diving into these dichotomies, we can view reciprocity broadly speaking as people's tendency to respond 'nicely' to actions they are in favour of and 'nastily' to those actions deemed unfavourable for them. If reciprocal feelings are strong, it means that people favour the relationship with others instead of pursuing their own self-interest, whereas if reciprocity is weak the self-interested notions have the upper hand within the proposed exchange (Guala, 2012).

Negative reciprocity is the result of getting something for nothing, for example, stealing (cf. Sahlins, 1972), whereas positive reciprocity enforces a common expectation of a positive contribution in return (for something given) regardless if it is in the form of a gift, a service, a compliment or a loan. Economists regard strong negative reciprocity differently; it is about incurring a cost to be able to inflict harm to others. If you have been wronged, you are willing to sacrifice resources in order to punish someone. It is seen as a trade-off between the pleasure of inflicting harm and the cost of punishment (Fehr et al., 2002; Reuben & van Winden, 2008).

Some scholars distinguish between vertical and horizontal reciprocity. The vertical variety of reciprocity illustrates the relationship between the public sector and taxpayers (Alm et al., 1993; Frey & Torgler, 2007; Bazart & Bonein, 2014). The horizontal variety describes the relationship between taxpayers themselves or between people having similar status. The vertical variety of reciprocity illustrates the relationship between the public sector and taxpayers and is by definition seen as unequal. Taxpayers may react to a disadvantageous or advantageous inequity through negative or positive reciprocal behaviours, respectively. A taxpayer's willingness to pay taxes increases—being positive—if they believe that other taxpayers also comply; and it will decrease—being negative—if the perception is that other taxpayers do not contribute their fair share. The reasons for taxpayers not contributing can be many: not understanding the law; stretching the law; outright cheating. But this negative sentiment directed towards other taxpayers can also have its origins in too complex tax laws or that they are fuzzily articulated. Here the negative reciprocity can be directed towards government. The same reciprocal reasoning about taxation can also be had regarding welfare services provided by government—that some taxpayers take advantage of the system or receive too much. These relationships have been researched as separate entities in studies of unfairness in taxation, yet as they are both potential sources of unfairness they ought to be studied in tandem (Schnellenbach, 2010; Bazart & Bonein, 2014).

Reciprocal ideas have been subject to the hypothesis that suggests taxpayers 'cheat' if they perceive that their money is not being well spent (Spicer & Lundstedt, 1976; Smith, 1992). A classic example of such reasoning is Henry David Thoreau's refusal to pay a poll tax, for which he was eventually put in jail.[1] It has been questioned whether his reason was that the American federal government did not abolish slavery (cf. Andreoni et al., 1998, p. 851) or if he was registering a protest against the

[1] http://historyofmassachusetts.org/henry-david-thoreau- arrested-for-nonpayment-of-poll-tax/

American–Mexican war; the point is that avoiding payment of tax can be, and has been, used as a protest against what taxpayers' money is spent on. Suggesting the modelling of such behaviour seems futile, although there are many attempts to do so—for example, a model of a dynamic and retrospective analysis of the relationship between government public good provision, government waste, considerations about fairness and taxpayer compliance has been proposed (Pommerehne et al., 1994).

Another distinction in reciprocity is between how taxpayers' money is collected and how this revenue is spent. There are numerous studies of how tax evasion is justified by reference to government expenditure; if I disagree with government policies—how tax money is spent—it makes sense to avoid paying up (Andreoni et al., 1998; Hanousek & Palda, 2004; Slemrod, 2007; Björklund Larsen, 2010). Such behaviour also depends on external circumstances—more taxation can be tolerated in times of warfare (Feldman & Slemrod, 2009) and the willingness to contribute is even increased, as recent studies of Ukraine under the Russian invasion has shown (Berenson & Birch, 2024).

Tax compliance research thus reveals a wide range of applications of reciprocity. Elsewhere, Björklund Larsen proposed four different ways in which reciprocity is applied in tax compliance research (2018). First, a *tit-for-tat relation* is to expect something in return for having given/paid a tribute to the state. This includes the disambiguation between various definitions of tit-for-tat: of earlier definitions of vengeful and negative reciprocal behaviour and the more recent definitions of getting something back. When it comes to taxes, there are time lags between giving and receiving something in return. But it cannot be too long; the time lag needs to be appropriate, otherwise it is just any market exchange. Second, a *copycat relation* means that a taxpayer does what other taxpayers do. It is learning by doing what others do. Third, taxpayers comply as they expect others to pay their *fair share*. If all taxpayers provide their fiscal contributions into the same coffer, all have paid. It is the collectivity of providing means for everybody's benefit. Reciprocity is here articulated as the explicit provision of taxes by all other taxpayers in a given society, and the implicit trust that taxes collected will also be distributed equally and fairly. Fourth, reciprocity as being *treated equally*; the scrutiny here is directed towards the power of the law and translation of the same into rules and regulations. There ought to be a reciprocal relationship despite the fact that there is an uneven distribution of power between the collector of taxes and those paying them. This is not only because of enforcement; tax law is by definition complicated, and the tax authority also has immense powers based on its public mission and its deep knowledge of applying tax law in practice.

These four categories of reciprocity obviously overlap. Wanting something for taxes paid does not have to be for individual benefit, but may indicate that such money ought to be spent on societal issues the taxpayer values and holds dear. A tit-for-tat expectation can go hand in hand with a feeling that other citizens should receive their fair share and be treated equitably.

Although hardly anyone pays taxes voluntarily, there is a recognition that if getting something for taxes paid, the willingness to comply increases. Some economists may have gone down the wrong path when they overlooked the reciprocal element in the willingness to comply and instead concentrated on the level of taxes paid and thus the propensity to being caught if avoiding paying tax (e.g. Allingham & Sandmo, 1972 and the plethora of succeeding research building on this assumption). Contradicting this, it has, for example, been shown that Swedes actually became more content with taxation from 1960 to 1980 despite the almost exponential increase in tax pressure during the period (Hadenius, 1985). Furthermore, in his huge research project regarding Swedish taxpayers' views on taxes (where 1200 respondents were interviewed for about 45 minutes each) and the usage of them, Hadenius noted:

> Strictly speaking, the replies given are inconsistent. Comparing the response to questions about tax levels and whether the subject's personal income tax is reasonable in view of the benefit derived from society reveals that 46 per cent gave contradictory replies: they think that the tax level is too high but at the same time consider the tax reasonable in relation to the benefit. (Hadenius, 1985, p. 353)

There is thus a plethora of approaches and explanations of the concept of reciprocity. And as reciprocity was something our participants repeatedly, albeit in various ways, returned to, we searched for ways to include this aspect in our four facets of belonging.

Turning to the perspective of taxpayers—citizens—and looking at the entire fiscal system, taxes can certainly be seen as containing reciprocal relations. Taxes have been provided by the individual—'taken fro' is perhaps more appropriate as most taxpayers do not have a choice—but there is clearly an expectation of receiving something in return, of relating to others receiving similar things and also making sure that we all contribute in some way.

To make a distinction between a taxpayer's rather transactional reasoning of fiscal belonging and compare it to more emotional and affective contributions, we propose a distinction: thick and thin reciprocity.

Concepts Thick and Thin

The term 'thick concept' has been attributed to the British philosopher Bernard Williams. In philosophy, there has been much debate about the nature of concepts with questions such as whether particular concepts are thick or thin as well as whether they are descriptive or evaluative, or whether they are evaluative or normative. For the British philosopher Bernard Williams, thick ethical concepts are 'reason giving concepts' whereas thin ethical concepts are general and abstract. In general terms, philosophers lean towards 'thin and cosmopolitan language that transcends local culture' (Williams, 1985, pp. 129–131, cited in O'Neill, 2005). This contrasts with anthropologists who seek to 'uncover a thick normative vocabulary that is local to particular cultures' (ibid.). This goes some way towards understanding anthropology's preference for 'thick description' (e.g. Geertz, 1973) seeking to uncover 'layers of interpretive depth' (O'Neill, 2005, p. 481). Thin descriptions merely describe physical behaviour, but they become thicker as more interpretive depth is added.

Neal Buckwalter and co-authors (2015), in the context of experimental philosophy, distinguish thin and thick beliefs. A thin belief is, in their view, a 'bare, cognitive pro-attitude' (ibid., p. 749) nothing more than a statement that something is true, without any emotional endorsement of its truth. A thick belief on the other hand requires more than thin belief; it also 'involves emotion or conation' (ibid.).

John O'Neill (2005) applies a thick and thin analysis to the concept of environmental values. He notes how international policy and treaties adopt thin scientific and market economic language that goes beyond the local to seek universal values that can be applied irrespective of local conditions.

In legal scholarship we can find extensive discussion of thin and thick versions of the rule of law, which is considered to be 'an elusive concept, the full contents of which are devoid of universal agreement' (Daly, 2024, p. 239). A thin account of the rule of law suggests that laws should provide guidance for citizens allowing them to 'know in advance the legal consequences that will follow' any course of action (Daly, 2021, p. 8). As Nick Cheesman notes, 'the thin rule of law is sometimes described as "rule by law"' (Cheesman, 2009; cf. Møller & Skaaning, 2012). Theorists of a thin rule of law are interested in how laws are created and enforced, i.e. the more formal aspects of law. A thick concept of the rule of law, on the other hand, is concerned with more than mere formalities and brings into play wider issues such as democracy and human rights.

The notion of 'thick reciprocity' and 'thin reciprocity', respectively, has to our knowledge mostly been applied in studies of local politics and community organisations to describe the extent of collaboration. Here is a definition of the thin variety:

> characterized by transactional interactions in which partners cooperate minimally with each other to achieve specific and often technical ends. In thinly reciprocal partnerships, partners are likely to invite others once into specific phases or activities of the project. While each partner may achieve the goal or outcome expected, they are not likely to have forged expectations, relationships, or other types of capacities required to initiate future or more complex and transformative collaborations. (Janke, 2013, p. 12, cf. Jameson et al., 2010)

Thin reciprocity is a practical and functional concept that facilitates cooperation and exchange in various spheres by aligning self-interest with mutual benefit, thus enabling structured and predictable interactions even in the absence of deeper social or emotional bonds. The concept seeks to explain the extent of engagement with others.

Our insights about thin and thick reciprocity thus take inspiration from several sources.

A New Way of Thinking About Reciprocity

Our fieldwork has led us to propose a continuum of forms of reciprocity. We do not see it as 'negative', 'balanced' and 'generalised' depending on which type of social relationships the exchanges take place within (Sahlins, 1972). It is more in the vein of being 'strong', where people favour the relationship with others instead of pursuing their own self-interest, or 'weak' when self-interested notions have the upper hand within the proposed exchange (Guala, 2012). However, to our mind, strong or weak are oppositional and relate more to power and intensity. Seeing reciprocity as vertical or horizontal takes us some way towards our goal but puts too much emphasis on the power relation. Thin and thick are more subtle descriptions and relate to size or width. As we are interested in finding a way to describe the reciprocal impact on the individual or on the collective the individual belongs to, we settle for thin and thick.

Thin Reciprocity

At one end of the continuum, reciprocity is quite instrumental; it is a tit-for-tat relation (Björklund Larsen, 2018) where you pay tax and note what you get for it. It is a narrow view of what taxes do for society, but especially in relation to yourself and your own contribution; it is close to a market exchange. Even if your tax contribution may be estimated, what you receive in return can never, ever be measured. Thin reciprocity is all about perceptions of getting something for taxes paid: in the past, now and in the future. The centre of attention in thin reciprocity is the individual taxpayer, perhaps extending to the immediate family.

Thin reciprocity closely relates to the economic theory of the actor in rational choice theory where the assumption is that individuals, or rational actors, actively aim to maximise their advantage in any situation. There is a clear link between payment of taxes and expectations about receiving public goods in return in the past or in the future.

Burt, born and raised in China, moved to the UK to pursue a master's degree, followed by a PhD. Having delivered some teaching whilst a PhD student, Burt discovered a passion for it and subsequently became an academic. Notwithstanding having lived in the UK for some 20 years, Burt identifies as Chinese, but also feels he belongs in the UK and is now a UK citizen.

Burt sees taxation as creating a reciprocal relation that creates a sense of belonging. He expresses himself as in debt; China gave him love, care and education which is more an emotional sense of gratefulness than that of the UK that has given him secondary education as well as learning from many other people. So for him it is pay-back time to the UK.

Yet, Burt also associates paying taxes with investing in the future for the benefit of his child: 'I think if I am making the contribution to the police, to the NHS and to the local city council, I think I'm also ensuring a better future for my child. I've tried to comfort myself by saying that it was an investment'. This is a reference to the social contract, and when asked what influences people's views on tax, Burt's response was that the key thing is 'what they get in return as the taxpayer and the public service'. He thus reinforces a thin, a fairly instrumental view of reciprocity.

Thick Reciprocity

Thick reciprocity is on the other hand more encompassing. It highlights that individuals recognise that taxes impact on society and culture. That taxes do something more than fulfil the immediate interest for the individual and perhaps their family.

Thick reciprocity can thus be:

> characterized by the mutual exchange of ideas, the collaborative generation of knowledge, shared power, and joint ownership of the full scope of work processes and outcomes. In thick reciprocal partnerships, partners share and shape ideas together in a generative and collaborative spirit. Thick reciprocity builds an understanding among partners and trusting relationships, the foundation for enduring and transformative partnerships. (Janke, 2013, p. 12)

Thick reciprocity creates a stronger social fabric where individuals feel secure and valued, knowing that their community or relationships are based on mutual respect, trust and a willingness to support each other through good times and bad. This concept helps build resilient and cohesive groups, fostering environments where cooperation and altruism thrive.

Our usage of thick reciprocity is also inspired by Clifford Geertz's notion of ethnography as being a 'thick description' of human behaviour (Geertz, 1973). When he depicted human social action, he could not just describe people's physical behaviours, but also in the context it was happening as interpreted by the actors. Although mainly a methodological point, a thick description of the role taxes play for our society can thereby be better understood by an outsider. A thick description typically adds a record of subjective explanations and meanings provided by the people engaged in the behaviours, making the collected data of greater value for studies by other social scientists. It is an interpretative analysis.

Thick reciprocity is thus more encompassing. It highlights that individuals recognise the impact of tax on society and culture—that taxes do something more than fulfil immediate interest for the individual, perhaps including their immediate family. With this type of reciprocity, we include the many and varied ways of building relations across society through taxes and taxation. Through our notion of thick reciprocity, we propose to shed light on the meaning our participants expressed when talking about taxes in relation to society—when they saw taxes as something more encompassing than addressing their own immediate needs.

Andrew came to Britain as a young teenage refugee separated from his family and thus came to Britain alone. An agent facilitated his arrival in the UK where he was dropped in London with no support. One of his first recollections on arrival was seeing a street beggar reading a book, leading him to think 'I so much want to be here', to be among a society where everyone can read books. With refugee status, Andrew was able to work while his application for leave to remain was processed, albeit for long hours and 'a very, very, very minimum wage', but proud to make a contribution to Britain at that age, rather than seek government benefits. A turning point for Andrew was when his London landlord recognised his talent for art and suggested he pursue a dream to become an architect in a different part of the country, outside of London, with a more homogeneous population. Andrew took this advice and subsequently pursued education and a career in education in a quieter part of the country.

Calling the UK home stems in part from moving at a moment in life when he started to shape his adult character. It was at the right moment when he was forced to leave his country of birth to look for a secure and good place to live. Andrew now thinks of himself as 'being a proud Brit' and became a citizen in 2005. His family was scattered, some in the UK and some in the USA, but growing up in Britain, receiving education and finding work led to Andrew feeling that he contributes to British society and is proud of his work as a professional educator.

In terms of tax, Andrew recognises that taxes are related to benefits received, not just financial but also moral. When asked how he feels about paying tax, Andrew's immediate response was 'happy, very happy', without questioning the amount of tax he is required to pay 'because, you know, there are people who work in this and you have to trust your government'. It is a sentiment stemming from the traditions of his family, in particular his parents. He feels educating the public about the benefits that society gets from paying taxes may shift the perception of it being a cost, in the same way as a utility bill is a cost, and which can be avoided.

Within this form of reciprocity, we include the many ways of building relations across society through taxes and taxation. If reciprocal relationships are an outcome of taxation, one could argue that reciprocity must be even more pertinent in states with high tax rates. This depends of course on how taxes are spent—what the taxpayer feels society gets for the money.

There are several explanations for why high tax rates have been accepted: because of war (e.g. Campbell, 1993; Feldman & Slemrod, 2009; Berenson & Birch, 2024), but also because of providing more public services. For example, as noted earlier Swedes actually became more content with taxation from 1960 to 1980 despite the almost exponential increase in tax pressure during that period (Hadenius, 1985, p. 362). They saw that the Swedish state provided them with increasing publicly funded services, e.g. thin reciprocity, but also that people across society became better off, e.g. thick reciprocity. Thick reciprocity is affective, creating a deep sentiment of recognising a state that has created a benevolent society. Thick reciprocity brushes away most of the transactional content of taxation; it is not much concerned with the amount of tax a person contributes, but recognises the gratefulness of living in the adopted society. Much of the research into tax compliance and willingness to pay tax brings into consideration a thin conception of reciprocity, one that is easier to measure through surveys and which resonates with respondents; of course they want 'bang for their buck' (D'Attoma, 2018). Yet there is a danger that, in doing so, societal issues are sidelined. A thicker, richer conception of reciprocity brings into consideration wider issues, including fiscal belonging. Yes, it is harder to 'measure', being related to emotion and feelings that are difficult to articulate, let alone to design measures to capture. Nonetheless, we believe that by acknowledging a thicker conception, we have the potential to greatly improve our understanding of why people pay taxes, which in turn can lead to better policies to encourage voluntary compliance with tax obligations.

Thin and Thick Reciprocity and the Four Facets of Belonging

It is important to note that any of the four facets cannot be reduced to either thin or thick reciprocity; instead, there is quality to each facet of thinner or thicker reciprocal sentiments. We provide a few examples below to illustrate how we consider this nuance.

Work

Throughout our engagement with the participants talking about tax, they mainly brought up income tax. As a second thought, other varieties of tax such as value added tax (VAT), national insurance contributions or the council tax were mentioned. Throughout, there was a heavy reliance on work as being the source for taxation. Katie, originally from Eastern Europe but both an American and a British citizen, is no fan of paying taxes and mainly relates her taxpaying to income from work in both countries. Each year she needs to declare her taxes in the USA which she finds ridiculous, whereas in the UK, she hardly notices the tax as 'it is all done automatically' (having its famous PAYE system) before she gets her pay cheque.

> I feel like it's like a necessary evil, but without that, like no one would just donate money to the schools or donate money to get the roads paved or streets cleaned. So it's like, I know it's a price you pay to live in the city and have the range of resources and things to access that the city provides for you, you know?

As she does not live or work in the USA, she finds it irritating to have to declare her income from another country (UK).

To work, earn an income and pay tax is an important facet of belonging to a society. A person does not only contribute fiscally through work, but being 'gainfully employed', they do not live off any public benefits either. We are also deeply embedded in the economic idea that creating a personal income is not only for ourselves; it also contributes to society's economic growth. Work is good and strengthens both the thin and thick aspects of reciprocity.

Family

Family seems immediately to be infused by thin reciprocity. It is about me and my closest relatives. Yet, a taxpayer can also want their children to grow up in a safe environment, like Burt did in the earlier example. He wants his son to have access to all infrastructure, safety and welfare British society provides. He wants him to grow up in an environment where he can get a good education. So family can also mean that taxes are not only for our immediate benefits, but rather to ensure that all will have access to the services in the future. So although the facet of family mainly relates to the thin reciprocal variety, it may also include that such services are given to the many, to compatriots, to a 'good' society (e.g. Gribnau et al., 2018).

Acceptance

Being accepted is relating to society beyond a person's closest human relations. It means feeling like anybody else in society. This builds heavily on thick reciprocity, of being accepted even if you by—ethnicity, race, religion, gender—belong to a minority.

When Peter, with his roots firmly planted in the Caribbean, thought about taxation, he related to how the UK government disburses the fiscal income. It was obvious how Peter remembered being treated by the police but also by other instances during his life; usually these were not happy memories. Peter is quite unhappy of the current organisation of tax payments in the UK. 'The tax system (VAT) does not benefit the ordinary working-class people. I think the tax burden is too much, because when you think of home, you've got grandparents and you have to help them, then seriously, you're cutting, as we say, back home'. Peter 'cuts' his UK tax contribution and instead uses it to help his grandparents. It is a different way to think about thick reciprocity; it is historical. In Peter's view immigrants' taxes should go to their country of origin because of that experience of colonialism, slavery, etc. These people and countries have often been economically exploited, in addition have their country of origin provided education etc. to the immigrant. The country of origin experiences a brain drain. The immigrant is now working and paying tax in the new country, so if/when they're paying tax, it should be paid to their country of origin.

Values

Recognising the values of a country and of society, whether cultural or political, mostly brings out the thick reciprocal aspect. For Alison, tax connects very much to her definition of a society as what we share, what we're doing together: 'Tax is a contribution to the services that we have decided that we want to have in common ... It's the glue for a nation. You can't have a nation without that tax'. But although she lived and worked most of her adult life in the UK, she is not comfortable with UK values. She says she resents some of the values of British society and especially the inherited privileges some have. She does not want to be a citizen as 'I'm not swearing my oath to king or queen'. Home is her Scandinavian country. It is where she is born, the country her values mainly connote. It is the transparency of the system she values and that has not changed from her move to the UK. Instead, her values of having a transparent system have even been intensified. 'There is not an openness I think the citizens should have because you build a society and you agree that these things should be what the state or the government provides'. Yet Alison belongs to the UK as she is married here. Alison's values in relation to that of the UK illustrate a fairly thin reciprocity.

Reflection

This chapter has explored how the concept of reciprocity enriches our understanding of taxation beyond its traditional definition as a compulsory, unrequited payment. Drawing on interdisciplinary perspectives and empirical fieldwork, the chapter reveals that many individuals perceive tax payment as a relational act—a way to give back, invest in the future and contribute to the social fabric. This sense of reciprocity can be categorised along a continuum from thin to thick. Thin reciprocity reflects instrumental, often individualistic motivation—taxes as a transactional exchange for public services. Thick reciprocity, in contrast, encompasses deeper emotional and moral commitments to the collective good, societal well-being and shared values.

Through the voices of diverse participants, the chapter illustrates how both forms of reciprocity intersect with facets of belonging such as work, family, acceptance and values. While thin reciprocity may dominate policy models and compliance research due to its measurability, the chapter argues that thick reciprocity—though harder to quantify—provides essential insights into civic solidarity, identity and moral engagement with both state and wider society. Ultimately, acknowledging the full spectrum of reciprocal sentiments offers a more nuanced and human-centred understanding of why people comply with tax systems and how taxation contributes to social cohesion and belonging. Thinking with tax as creating reciprocal relations brings us a long way from the textbook definition of tax as a compulsory, unrequited payment.

References

Allingham, M. G., and A. Sandmo. 1972. Income tax evasion: A theoretical analysis. *Journal of Public Economics* 1 (3–4): 323–338. http://scholar.google.se/scholar?hl=sv&q=sandmo%2C+agnar&btnG=#0.

Alm, J. 2012. Measuring, explaining, and controlling tax evasion: Lessons from theory, experiments, and field studies. *International Tax and Public Finance* 19 (1): 54–77. http://link.springer.com/article/10.1007/s10797-011-9171-2.

Alm, J., R. Bahl, and M. N. Murray. 1993. Audit selection and income tax underreporting in the tax compliance game. *Journal of Development Economics* 42 (1): 1–33. https://www.sciencedirect.com/science/article/pii/0304387893900704.

Andreoni, J., B. Erard, and J. Feinstein. 1998. Tax compliance. *Journal of Economic Literature* 36 (2): 818–860. https://www.jstor.org/stable/2565123.

Bazart, C., and A. Bonein. 2014. Reciprocal relationships in tax compliance decisions. *Journal of Economic Psychology* 40:83–102. https://doi.org/10.1016/j.joep.2012.10.002.

Berenson, M. P., & Birch, S. (2024). *How do wars make states ? Institutional trust and attitudes toward tax compliance in wartime Ukraine.* Presentation at Annual Meeting of the American Political Science Association, August–September 2024.

Björklund Larsen, L. (2010). *Illegal yet licit: Justifying informal purchases of work in contemporary Sweden* [Stockholm Studies in Social Anthropology, Acta Universitatis Stockholmiensis]. http://su.diva-portal.org/smash/record.jsf?pid=diva2:287414

Björklund Larsen, L. 2018. *A fair share of tax. A fiscal anthropology of contemporary Sweden.* Palgrave Macmillan.

Buckwalter, W., D. Rose, and J. Turri. 2015. Belief through thick and thin. *Noûs* 49 (4): 748–775. https://doi.org/10.1111/nous.12048.

Campbell, J. L. 1993. The state and fiscal sociology. *Annual Review of Sociology* 163–185.

Cheesman, N. 2009. Thin rule of law or un-rule of law in Myanmar? *Pacific Affairs* 82 (4): 597–613. https://doi.org/10.5509/2009824597.

D'Attoma, J. 2018. More bang for your buck: Tax compliance in the United States and Italy. *Journal of Public Policy* 40 (1): 1–24. https://doi.org/10.1017/S0143814X18000302.

Daly, S. 2021. The rule of (soft) law. *King's Law Journal* 32 (1): 3–13. https://doi.org/10.1080/09615768.2021.1885326.

Daly, S. 2024. Artificial intelligence, the rule of law and public administration: The case of taxation. *Cambridge Law Journal* 83 (April 2024): 437–464. https://doi.org/10.1017/S0008197324000448.

Encyclopaedia Britannica. (n.d.). *Britannica.* https://www.britannica.com. Retrieved December 2, 2024.

Fehr, E., and A. Falk. 2002. Psychological foundations of incentives. *European Economic Review* 46 (4–5): 687–724. https://www.sciencedirect.com/science/article/pii/S0014292101002082.

Fehr, E., U. Fischbacher, and S. Gächter. 2002. Strong reciprocity, human cooperation, and the enforcement of social norms. *Human Nature* 13 (1): 1–25.

Feldman, N. E., and J. Slemrod. 2009. War and taxation: When does patriotism overcome the free-rider impulse? In *The new fiscal sociology: Taxation in comparative and historical perspective*, ed. I. W. Martin, A. K. Mehrotra, and M. Prasad, 138–154. Cambridge University Press.

Frey, B. S., and B. Torgler. 2007. Tax morale and conditional cooperation. *Journal of Comparative Economics* 35 (1): 136–159. https://www.sciencedirect.com/science/article/pii/S0147596706000849.

Geertz, C. 1973. *The interpretation of cultures.* Basic Books.

Gribnau, H. (2013). Legal certainty: A matter of principle (*Tilburg Law School Legal Studies Research Paper Series* No.12). http://papers.ssrn.com/sol3/papers.cfm?abstract_id=2447386

Gribnau, H. 2015. Taxation, reciprocity and communicative regulation. *Tilburg Law Review* 20 (2): 191–212. http://booksandjournals.brillonline.com/content/journals/10.1163/22112596-02002009.

Gribnau, H., E. van der Enden, and K. Baisalbayeva. 2018. Codes of conduct as a means to manage ethical tax governance. *Intertax* 46 (5): 390–407. https://doi.org/10.54648/taxi2018040.

Guala, F. 2012. Reciprocity: Weak or strong? What punishment experiments do (and do not) demonstrate. *Behavioral and Brain Sciences* 35 (1): 1–15. https://doi.org/10.1017/S0140525X11000069.

Hadenius, A. 1985. Citizens strike a balance: Discontent with taxes, content with spending. *Journal of Public Policy* 5 (3): 349–363. http://journals.cambridge.org/abstract_S0143814X00003159.

Hanousek, J., and F. Palda. 2004. Quality of government services and the civic duty to pay taxes in the Czech and Slovak republics, and other transition countries. *Kyklos* 57 (2): 237–252. http://onlinelibrary.wiley.com/doi/10.1111/j.0023-5962.2004.00252.x/full.

Jameson, J., P. Clayton, and A. Jaeger. 2010. Community engaged scholarship as mutually transformative partnerships. In *Participatory partnerships for social action and research*, ed. L. Harter, J. Hamel-Lambert, and J. Millesen, 259–277. Dubuque, IA: Kendall Hunt.

Janke, E. 2013. Increased community presence is not a proxy for reciprocity. *EJournal of Public Affairs* 2 (2).

Keen, M., and J. Slemrod. 2021. *Rebellion, rascals, and revenue tax follies and wisdom through the ages.* Princeton University Press.

Kirchler, E. 1998. Differential representations of taxes: Analysis of free associations and judgments of five employment groups. *Journal of Socio-Economics* 27 (1): 117–131.

Kornhauser, M. E. 2007. A tax morale approach to compliance: Recommendations for the IRS. *Florida Tax Review* 8 (6): 599–634. http://heinonlinebackup.com/hol-cgi-bin/get_pdf.cgi?handle=hein.journals/ftaxr8&section=27.

Leroy, M. 2008. Tax sociology sociopolitical issues for a dialogue with economists. *Socio-Logos. Revue de l'association Francaise de Sociologie* 3 (3): 1–28.

Møller, J., and S.-E. Skaaning. 2012. Systematizing thin and thick conceptions of the rule of law. *The Justice System Journal* 33 (2): 136–153.

O'Neill, J. 2005. Environmental values through thick and thin. *Conservation and Society* 3 (2): 479–500.

Pommerehne, W. W., A. Hart, and B. S. Frey. 1994. Tax morale, tax evasion and the choice of policy instruments in different political systems. *Public Finance* 49 (Supplement): 52–69.

Rabin, M. 1998. Psychology and economics. *Journal of Economic Literature* 36: 11–46. https://www.jstor.org/stable/2564950.

Reuben, E., and F. van Winden. 2008. Social ties and coordination on negative reciprocity: The role of affect. *Journal of Public Economics* 92 (1–2): 34–53. https://doi.org/10.1016/j.jpubeco.2007.04.012.

Sahlins, M. D. 1972. *Stone age economics*. Routledge.

Schnellenbach, J. 2010. Vertical and horizontal reciprocity in a theory of taxpayer compliance. In *Developing alternative frameworks for explaining tax compliance*, ed. J. Alm, J. Martinez-Vasquez, and B. Torgler, 56–73. Routledge International Studies in Money and Banking.

Slemrod, J. B. 1992. *Why people pay taxes: Tax compliance and enforcement*. University of Michigan Press.

Slemrod, J. B. 2007. Cheating ourselves: The economics of tax evasion. *Journal of Economic Perspectives* 21 (1): 25–48. https://www.jstor.org/stable/30033700.

Smith, K. W. 1992. Reciprocity and fairness: Positive incentives for tax compliance. In *Why people pay taxes, tax compliance and enforcement*, ed. J. B. Slemrod, 223–250. University of Michigan Press.

Spicer, M. W., and S. B. Lundstedt. 1976. Understanding tax evasion. *Public Finance* 31 (2): 295–305.

Westerman, P. 2014. Reciprocity: A fragile equilibrium. *Netherlands Journal of Legal Philosophy* 2 (43): 172–184.

Williams, B. 1985. *Ethics and the limits of philosophy*. Fontana.

CHAPTER 6

Fiscal Culture

Abstract The concept of *fiscal culture* provides an overarching approach to understanding how people see the connection between taxes collected and public spending. Taking a critical perspective on fiscal culture highlights how taxpayer behaviour is seldom described by static categories such as nationality, country of origin, being native or an immigrant, gender, etc. Instead, it allows us to provide a more holistic perspective and see how they relate to both paying taxes and receiving benefits from them. First we review some important work on one side of it—that of tax culture. We then illustrate with a few important anthropological studies of the notion of culture, one of the most central concepts in the discipline. We end the chapter by looking at how fiscal culture can be applied to Paulina's narrative, born and educated in South American and now working as a human rights lawyer in London.

Keywords Tax culture • Concept of culture • Fiscal culture • Anthropology

> I can see that whatever contribution I make, one way or another it is coming back to me and I'm happy for that. Yeah, it's something I never had in the past where I come from.
>
> —Paulina, born and raised in South America.

L. Björklund Larsen, L. Oats, *Crossing Borders, Sharing Burdens*,
https://doi.org/10.1007/978-3-031-99394-7_6

Tax Culture

That tax cultures are national is an easy connotation. Legal distinctions of tax are almost exclusively national, and taxation has historically mostly addressed activities taking place inside the geographical borders of a nation. Taxation is most often imposed by a national public authority applying national laws, yet in praxis, these laws may be applied at federal, regional or municipal level. Yet there is an increasing amount of international tax work that has potential to influence national practices. Organisations such as the Organisation for Economic Co-operation and Development (OECD) advocate for international collaboration initiatives, and there are increasing amounts of data and other exchanges of information between national tax administrations designed to improve compliance and thwart tax evasion. There are many actors in the global tax arena that impose rules, regulations and data on national tax systems with a view to changing tax cultures. We need to rethink tax culture.

Culture can broadly be defined as learnt and shared beliefs and behaviours among those that are seen to *belong* to the given culture. Yet the concept of culture in tax research is often taken for granted or seems to be a collector of what cannot be explained by other concepts. When not properly defined, 'it is cultural' makes the concept a container for the irrational, the strange, the difficult to measure and even the exotic. This is unfair to the substantial research on the culture concept itself. Defining, understanding and analysing culture(s) came out of an ambition to understand why groups of people in the world were so different—not in looks but in beliefs, behaviour, family relationships or how these were integrated into modes of survival; what we often call the economy. That people share a culture has often been colloquially equated with nations; we talk about Afghani, Brazilian, Chinese or Danish culture. Yet even within nations, there is an extraordinary diversity of human ways of living and of living together.

There are quite a few studies of 'tax cultures' and 'cultures of taxation'. What is noteworthy is the difference in focus between tax as a set of written laws, rules and regulations, how these are all set in motion in organisations and in society and people's reaction to those. We suggest four ways in which tax cultures have been used in the literature.

First, *reacting to change* consists mainly of descriptive studies where culture is used to explain taxpayers' reaction to changes in tax systems. The cultural aspect often comes across as behaviour that does not fit into existing models. Birger Nerrè's (2008) study aimed to take culture seriously in tax research, and not just as a residual for irrational behaviour. He proposed interesting concepts such as *tax culture shocks* and *tax culture lags*, which recognise the importance of tax-collectors' administrative burdens while paying attention to how taxpayers react to change, especially recognising tax rate rises. Yet, his economic-historical focus was strictly national and the examples were based on two nations, Japan after WWII and post-Soviet Russia in the 1990s that at the time had economies in considerable disarray. Research and understanding of organisations as being cultural drawing on anthropological research started in the 1980s. Linda Smircich underlined that such a usage of the concept of culture made it possible to question 'taken-for-granted assumptions, raising issues of context and meaning, and bringing to the surface underlying values' (1983, p. 355). Thus different varieties of 'culture' could address a variety of problems. An example of such an analysis is Sara Closs-Davies and co-authors' investigation of how accounting technologies at HMRC (His Majesty's Revenue and Customs) transformed public values (2020). They draw attention to how new ideas about organisation—new public management as it were—change both employees' behaviour and relations with the taxpayers they ought to serve. They refer to 'workplace culture', 'organisational culture' and 'quantification culture', but we as readers need to imagine how these 'cultures' are defined and how they relate to each other. If part of a culture is how we speak about issues, there are indeed events that change the public discourse, for example, when the Panama papers and the Paradise papers were revealed. Gertrud, a Scandinavian whose entire professional life has been in the UK, hints at a shift in tax culture when she commented:

> But now we question if it is morally right to avoid paying tax. The release of the Panama Papers and now the next level of papers and all the people being exposed by them show that they have not necessarily broken laws, but acted in a way that [other] people think is morally wrong. And that never used to be a point that people said a few years ago.

Second, *taxation in practice* is based on how taxation operates in the real world. Focus is thus on fiscal collection and organisation, often offering a comparative or historical perspective. Ann Mumford, a legal scholar, used tax cultures to explore why the methods of collecting tax in the UK and the US differed (2002). Sven Steinmo and his contributors take an institutional perspective and note how the relationship between taxpayer and tax collector has evolved over time in a comparison of Italy, Romania, Sweden, the UK and the USA (2018). The aim is to understand how broader social, political and even cultural contexts structure and inform individual tax decisions. We find more inspiration in Raymond Atuguba's approach on tax cultures in his native Ghana (2021). He argues that tax administrations that aim to increase voluntary compliance ought to think holistically about society. Such an approach needs to include taxpayers' understanding of the history, tax laws, information and education about tax, how revenue authorities collect taxes, how transparent the system is and how any disputes are resolved, how satisfied taxpayers are and finally the extent to which taxes are avoided. As one of our participants observes:

> It's people, people's traditions, sort of their tradition, their tradition as it relates to taxpaying. How people feel about taxpaying and whether or not they think that there should be certain taxes. It regards how tax affects them, whether or not they should pay tax and so on. That is how important and significant they considered tax to be. (George, originally from the Caribbean)

Molly, originally from Scandinavia, sees a tax culture as a 'collective set of practices around tax. I feel like my home country has a much stronger tax culture than the UK has'. And she adds, 'It's about feelings, it's about infrastructure, it's about figures'. A tax culture is thus not only descriptive, it is about getting something for taxes paid and it regards how much you pay in tax. Such tax culture is somehow evaluated in terms of being strong or weak. Yet it also includes avoidance strategies. Molly adds: 'Here [there] is more of an established route for how people can avoid taxation ... UK does, in that sense, have a tax culture of wealthy people moving money abroad'.[1]

Third, *models of and models for* follows a Geertzian view on culture (1973).[2] When culture is used as a 'model of' the social world, it reflects back on the reality that specific social worlds have produced.

[1] For a more detailed description of Scandinavian taxation, see, for example, Karen Boll's work on the Danish Tax and Customs Administration (Boll, 2014) and Björklund Larsen's (2017) book on the Swedish Tax Administration (STA). She argues that the STA takes a lot of steps aiming to shape taxpayers but are also shaped by values held by them.

[2] Clifford Geertz was an American anthropologist. He had an enormous influence on the discipline, and beyond, in the 1960–1980s period. One of his contributions was arguing for the need of 'Thick description', to explain with as much detail as possible the reason behind human actions. A human action can mean many different things, and Geertz insisted that scholars need to be aware of this.

Correspondingly, 'models for' social worlds produce a reality that the model of social worlds describes. The models of and models for thus reiterate and complement each other. Michael Livingston, a legal scholar, has worked with 'tax culture' for a long time (2005; 2020). He is interested in the definition of a 'tax culture' and asks: do we mean attitudes or institutions or a combination of the two, or is it perhaps a result of a country's legal culture (2020, p. 9)? He argues that the notion of a global tax culture has emerged out of the economics discipline that assumes that all tax systems can be evaluated in the same way. Yet, he shows that national tax systems have different goals and as such pursue different values. For example, the Dutch are said to have a tax culture where tax legislature fosters a rule-based mindset focused on tax planning (Gribnau, 2015, p. 232). Assaf Likhovski's premise is that culture and law are mutually constitutive (2011, p. 849) and more specifically that we continuously re-articulate legal and cultural meanings in a loop. Ruth Braunstein proposes a theory of cultural dynamics drawing on distinctions between the sacred, the profane and the mundane. A *taxpaying culture,* in the USA, consists of laws but also the public debates, people's attitudes, materialities and everyday tax practices (Braunstein, 2024). In her analysis religious convictions play a large role.

A culture consists of the non-material issues—shared ideas, beliefs, symbols, values, social norms and practices—that bind people together. These issues are often grounded in history and in tradition but are distinct from power. It is noteworthy that the models of and models for a view on culture are also susceptible to change (as discussed in the first way tax cultures are used). Does the aftermath of the public outrage that the Panama and Paradise papers created make possible numerous international initiatives such as the minimum global corporate tax of 15% recently introduced for large multinationals?

Fourth, a *positive view of culture* where tax compliance is by definition good tax behaviour. This is the approach taken by the OECD advising tax administrations on how to educate taxpayers (2015 [2021]). They provide examples from tax administrations and other public institutions around the world. Anne, a young woman from Northern Europe, illustrates this view: 'I would describe a tax culture as the general population's willingness to respect and cooperate with those paying their tax, I guess, and that general societal understanding of why they are there'. The notion of culture thus easily connects to the national definition. The stronger the culture, the stronger tax compliance. Policy studies such as those produced by the OECD omit the diversity of tax behaviour—that it also includes avoiding, omitting, cheating, evading, making mistakes etc. These attempts to describe what a tax culture is draw our attention to very different contexts. There is the recognition that cultures can exist beyond the nation and that it is a concept that is somewhat in motion and subject to change. Tax cultures can be changed. The difficult issue is deciding what to change. A tax culture has been described as strong (Bergman, 2003; Kuandykov et al., 2021; OECD, 2015 [2021]), healthy (Evans, 2017; Gaber & Gruevski, 2018; Saleheen, 2013) and low (Kuandykov et al., 2021) and is as such implicitly measured, but still more or less taken for granted.

It is noteworthy that we can also have a strong tax evasive culture (Ordower, 2010; Sánchez Román, 2013). Our participants agree with the latter. Nina talks about how she sees tax in her parents' home country:

> [L]ike in my country in Eastern Europe, it would be much more prevalent to kind of drop the VAT off some bill or something like that. And everyone will wink, wink and have a beer and celebrate the fact they got away with it. And it's just not a kind of taboo in that way. And that doesn't mean that everyone's trying to avoid paying as much tax as possible. But, there's a whole other kind of sentiment around it. It's about doing favours with your friends and things like that.[3] So I think it's just sort of connected to different logics: economic logics, moral logics and so forth.

Colleen, from the Caribbean, had a similar reflection on opportunities for non-compliance among those engaged in the informal economy[4]: 'In my home country probably more than half of the taxpaying population are engaged in the informal economy. There seems to be a natural disposition not to pay tax there, even by persons who are employed in the formal system'.

[3] Favours here are those that have a value and potentially could be subject to tax assessment.

[4] The concept of the *informal economy* was coined by the anthropologist Keith Hart in the early 1970s and has been widely used both in academia and in practice since. The informal economy is defined as 'the mass of economic transactions that takes place beyond effective state regulation' (Hart, 2001, p. 98). When Hart did fieldwork amongst immigrants in Ghana's capital Accra, he observed that individuals were very busy living, working and surviving, although officially Ghana had an enormous unemployment rate (Hart, 1973). What he described as the informal economy was made up of survival strategies by poor people where authorities were deemed to be a threat. He emphasised the wish to avoid bureaucracy, especially regarding taxation, but also regulations and official records.

There are thus many inspirational studies of tax cultures that go beyond national boundaries, irrational behaviour or the realm of specific societal institutions. Yet, what makes up a tax culture can be many things. Although most of our participants have a leaning towards seeing a tax culture shaped by how it is put into practice, there are also scholars that see different aspects. As fiscal anthropologist Greg Rawlings wrote:

> [S]ocial life is fundamentally concerned with the makings and meanings of culture, which can often be most eloquently expressed in narrative form. These same structures and nuances of meaning have relevance in contemporary nation-states and as such anthropology may well be able to play an important 'fiscal role' in exploring the nuances and complexities of taxation and compliance in the twenty-first century. (Rawlings, 2003, p. 277)

Cultures matter for how tax is legislated, practised, applied and reacted to. Before defining how we regard/define a fiscal culture, we take a step backwards to see how cultures can be understood using anthropological definitions.

Culture

How to define a culture to which people belong? In the following we draw on the discipline of anthropology, as culture is one of the most central, yet also hotly debated, concepts in anthropological research. Culture has a long history.

Edward Tylor (1871) was apparently first to provide a formal description of *culture*. He defined it as '[t]hat complex whole which includes knowledge, belief, art, morals, law, custom, and any other capabilities and habits acquired by man as a member of society'. Yet, anthropologists' focus at the time was on people living elsewhere and otherwise, and shed light on different ways of living by being there (Boas, 1897; Malinowski, 1922a, 1922b). The people that were studied usually lived in isolated and faraway places and led very different lives compared to the anthropologist studying them. Focus was on 'the other/s' (e.g. Fabian, 1983) and the way anthropologists depicted ways of living for a group of people was called a culture. Historically, there has been an evolution of both the concept and definition of culture and how it was studied. What follows are three significant contributions to how anthropologists have approached it and what we can learn from each contribution.

Tim Ingold proposed four stages of defining culture in a historical narrative (Ingold, 1994), an illustration of how the understanding of the concept has changed over time. First, culture was seen in terms of evolution and degree of civilisation. It was an imaginary comparison to the anthropologist's own culture/society trying to draw historical traits creating stepping-stones in an *evolutionary staircase* towards 'civilised', modern, Western societies. The argument went that a group of people often referred to as a tribe, who were living primitively would at some future point evolve and become more like contemporary society in which the reporting anthropologist lived. Second, realising that there were other differences between ways of living than understanding them through evolutionary steps, a *relativistic view* of culture slowly took over. Cultures were depicted, where each represented a traditional way of living consisting of customary behaviour, institutions and using particular artefacts. Such studies were still mostly confined to a specific geographical site where the behaviour of people could only be judged in relation to their specific values and standards. Third, trying to understand how societies/cultures were subject to change and why they had developed so differently, a more *structural understanding* was introduced. In each culture described, anthropologists attempted to find underlying structures that had symbolic meaning. Culture was in this perspective put in opposition to behaviour, much as language was opposed to speech. A culture could be defined in terms of a shared system of concepts such as kinship relations, religious beliefs, economic structures and language, which were inherited and reproduced. Fourth, more recognition was given to individual behaviour shaping cultures. Nowadays cultures are often studied as the outcome, the result, of *human practices within a community* be it a suburb, a digital world or a professional setting. An anthropologist follows people in order to see how they are involved and engaged in such social world(s). It is a depiction of what people do in relation to other people and what people do in relation to what they write and say.

There are two important insights from this very brief and sketchy trajectory of understanding cultures. First, there is no established meaning and proper definition of culture. As in Tylor's celebrated definition, culture includes all 'capabilities and habits acquired by man as a member of society' (1871, p. 1). Each and every one might put diverse emphasis on different aspects of what it means to be human as part of a culture. Second, regardless of how we define culture, we can never encounter culture on the ground. The world is not made up of a nice patchwork of different cultures existing side by side in the world, ready to be asked about, surveyed, described and thus measured as Hofstede proposed (2011)[5] and by which much of the research on tax culture as described above is inspired. 'People *live culturally* rather than that they *live in cultures*', wrote Tim Ingold (1994, p. 331). The implication is that asking what is 'your tax culture' is meaningless. It is not there to be easily sought and deduced, it has to be interpreted and understood through thorough ethnographic engagement. 'The concept of culture entails a high level of abstraction' (ibid., p. 330).

Arjun Appadurai stresses the semantic difference between culture the noun and cultural the adjective. Here the focus is on the changing nature of 'culture(s)'. When we propose that people live in a culture, it becomes an object or a thing; it makes it static. Furthermore, it excludes many other instances of social inequality such as race, education and lifestyle. Culture as a noun 'begins to smack of any variety of biologisms' (Appadurai, 1996, p. 12) and risks hiding more than it reveals (implied by many of the tax culture definitions referred to above). Instead, people live culturally. It is an approach that highlights points of similarity and difference between static categories such as class, gender, role, group and nation (ibid.). The cultural aspect thus provides another dimension, a distinction as to what it means to belong to a group. Culture is a heuristic that allows us to talk about differences between social categories (ibid., p. 13) in a globalised world.

Ulf Hannerz has avidly addressed the issue of culture and has especially been concerned with how culture can be understood when people move around. Addressing how migration makes an impact on cultures, Hannerz suggested *creolization* as a concept (Hannerz, 1987). In his fieldwork in Nigeria, he saw how Nigerians who had been living in the UK, or had

[5] Geert Hofstede has been immensely influential with his ideas about nationalistic cultures and has inspired much management and business literature but also tax research. It is therefore important to underline some of the hazards of using his dimensions. He defines culture as 'the collective programming of the mind that distinguishes the members of one group or category of people from others' (Hofstede, 2011). Hofstede's dimensions are validated statistically and thus have a 'scientific appeal' to many researchers. There are many objections to studying culture by conducting quantitative surveys, analyse answers statistically with the results collated into numerical indices and matrices. A simplistic notion of 'culture' such as Hofstede's may become an entity with its own property that resides in people's minds (Dahlén, 1997) or simplistically equates nation with culture (Baskerville, 2003). As such, Hofstede's 'culture' has very little if nothing at all to do with identifying a culture, or studying it qualitatively.

friends and relatives there, brought back British ways of doing and being. Back in Nigeria, they amalgamated new traditions with old ones, finding new and creative expressions. Like the Caribbean language, these people draw on different sources. The concept of culture as an instrument provides 'adaptations and reactions to a given situation rather than as a completely autonomous determinant of behavior' (Hannerz, 1969, p. 193). An analysis of culture is thus 'a study of the way people develop a culture as an instrument for coping with their conditions of life' (Hannerz, 2019, p. 62). This also means that a culture does not need to be homogenous or specifically coherent. Throughout his career, Hannerz has continued to challenge us, proposing that culture can be both the 'replication of uniformity' (Hannerz, 2016, p. 143) and an 'organisation of diversity' (ibid.). The creolisation process looks immediately promising when we consider how our participants relate to taxes. Yet, as we will argue, there are other more prominent issues at play.

Hannerz has more broadly addressed the meaning of cultures in contemporary life (Hannerz, 2016). He proposes that there are four different organisational settings—what he calls frames—where people handle meanings. These four frames are states, markets, movements and 'consociality'. States and markets are easy to understand and are often set in opposition to each other. Market behaviour has during the last 30 years been seen to intrude on our understanding of what the state is as expressed in ideas such as 'New Public Management'. Yet markets are most often the source for taxation; this is where commodities and services are exchanged and based on the exchange value can be taxed. Movements need more explanation but often consist of fluctuating ideas around which people gather. 'Movements try to mobilise people for some common goal, either because something valued in the present faces a threat, or because something better can be envisaged for the future' (Hannerz, 2016, p. 147). Finally, consociality encompasses all interactions between people in different settings. This can be within the family, how strangers interact on sidewalks in big-city streets, contacts between friends and acquaintances, how colleagues at work interact, relations between neighbours, etc. An intermediate conclusion based on the four organisational frames is that cultures are always a 'work in progress' and a result of people adapting to particular conditions and events.

We use the above insights when we propose a way to consider fiscal culture.

From Tax Culture to Fiscal Culture

One way to address the connection between welfare and taxes is to move from tax culture to fiscal culture. We argue that the link here is the flip side of revenue collection, that is, government spending. It is the link between these two fiscal activities that is at the heart of reciprocity, as we saw in the previous chapter, which animates many discussions about tax yet is analysed as a distinct phenomenon. Fiscal culture in this view is an amalgam of tax culture and spending culture.

Strangely enough, there is little research addressing the connection between taxing and spending, but we do find glimpses of an overlap between these two areas of scholarship in work that deals with the phenomenon of tax expenditures. Åsa Gunnarsson (2020) observed that the typologies of welfare states (as developed, for example, by Esping-Andersen, 1990) do not capture the tax dimension of welfare provision. The funding of welfare commitments is largely neglected in welfare state research. She argues that classifications of welfare states and classifications of 'families of taxation' need more comprehensive theoretical perspectives to move beyond the current fragmented picture.

Tax expenditures are essentially tax revenue foregone in order to foster social and other objectives through the tax system rather than via direct payments, for example, as welfare. Most of the research on tax expenditures is conducted by tax scholars; indeed, neglect of tax among social and welfare policy scholars is puzzling if not alarming. This is particularly so because in popular discourse, tax culture and welfare culture are two sides of the same coin. Who pays taxes and who receives welfare and other benefits are often discussed together, yet in scholarship the two practices of collecting and spending are seldom addressed.

A fiscal culture thus illustrates how people see the connection between taxes and government spending. Just thinking about this relation underlines that a fiscal culture is seldom described by static categories such as by nationality, by country of origin, by being native or an immigrant, by gender, etc. Instead, it is how people more holistically relate to both paying taxes and receiving benefits from them. What is important in this perspective is that fiscal culture is constantly in motion; *we live culturally* following Appadurai's point. Proposing a fiscal culture is thus not to suggest a static and clearly identified culture composed of specific views and practices on taxes and public expenditure. Instead, we draw on Hannerz's four organisational frames that make up a fiscal culture: state, market, movement and consociality.

First, it is through the state that tax laws are made and so are the tax collecting authorities. They are instituted by the state to conduct the fiscal task of collecting tax revenue. Such authorities follow rules and regulations but have also considerable room to organise how the fiscal collection should be conducted. They introduce compliance strategies, choose taxpayers to audit, go digital in various ways. It is also through the state that public expenditure and welfare are distributed. The frame of the state plays a large role in a fiscal culture.

Second, the market creates objects, things, services: being in the market they are granted value when exchanged—and can thus become subject to tax. It is also through the market that many people earn their living. They are employed or conduct their own business. The state taxes the market—notably in the UK through value added tax (VAT) but also with many other taxes and excise duties—but people understand that it is through the market that values are created, values that can be taxed.

Movement provides a third frame to analyse how people come together for a common goal. It is about how ideas mobilise people. It is noteworthy that movement is not about migration per se, but can instead illustrate how ideas spread about other ways of doing things. Tax authorities collaborate across national borders, both learning from each other's strategies. There are international collaborations through the OECD, TAXUD, Fiscalis,[6] etc. Tax authorities also exchange information about taxpayers that have international activities and earnings; these can include ideas on tax compliance, tax avoidance, tax planning, etc. More importantly, ideas about strategies for taxpayers travel. Those who wish to plan, avoid or even evade taxes find rich inspiration facilitated by specialised tax advisers.

Finally, consociality provides a frame for how people relate to each other—to other taxpayers—through thinking with tax. If services are paid for from the public purse, people might not need the help of family, friends and neighbours. That is, people live in a welfare state. But if there is a need to get help from other people in order to survive and make do, the consociality frame in a fiscal culture is more important. It is noteworthy that if

[6] OECD is the Organisation for Economic Co-operation and Development. TAXUD stands for Directorate-General for Taxation and Customs Union in the European Union. Fiscalis is an EU cooperation programme that enables national tax administrations to create and exchange information and expertise. It helps Member States develop and run major trans-European information technology tax systems, as well as establishing networks of officials across the EU. This includes fighting tax fraud, tax evasion and tax avoidance, and improving tax collection.

the state changes its provision of welfare services, consociality will also change but not always in the opposite direction. Shrinking public welfare might increase the need to rely on other people and the consociality frame might take a more prominent place in fiscal culture, but if public expenditure on culture is increased so might be the importance of the consociality frame.

Before diving into an example of how we can understand a fiscal culture, it is important to recall that the organisational frames do not work in separation from each other.

Fiscal Culture Applied: Paulina

Paulina came from South America to the UK to take a master's degree in law. Love happened, she met her future husband—a native Brit—and is now married with two kids, happily residing in a London suburb and working as a human rights lawyer. We use her story to illustrate ethnographically how a fiscal culture can be understood.

Paulina presents herself as British-South American. She still sees her native country in South America as her home country but says that she feels much, much more comfortable living in this suburb of London and in the UK. She has made friendships and so have her kids, she describes them as really strong friendships. These friendships are very important for her being away from her own family at home. She really feels she belongs to the environment and she likes the schools they go to. This is where she wants her kids to grow up; she thinks she would have liked to have had such an environment when she was a child. She is now a UK citizen, not by explicit choice but because it is just easier when crossing borders. It was a freedom issue. Once returning back from South America, before getting her passport, she had a dreadful experience at UK customs:

> They didn't even believe that I was legally married, so they held me at the airport for a few hours. They investigated my references, my academic record and they even contacted my dissertation supervisor. It was quite an awful experience. After having gone through that, I understood that the best solution was to become a citizen to avoid having to come through separate entrances [at the airport].

Being a British citizen means, however, that she has to pay immigration duties when entering her native country. That is an economic drawback, but worth it.

Paulina says that she pays taxes in both countries.

> I pay taxes in the UK. But when I'm home, I also pay taxes. I try to mainly use the services, the shopping, whatever I need to do, in the regulated places because I know how tough the informal market can be in my country.

It is noteworthy that she stills speaks about her native country as 'home'. There is a huge informal market where products and services are obviously cheaper than on the formal one. She says that she wants to contribute to building a formal society for other compatriots, although she is not particularly keen on the governing state. When she grew up the government was harsh on political dissidents. Her parents had been living through various periods of dictatorships and she grew up knowing that restrictions were not only on freedom of movement. There were also restrictions regarding freedom of speech, freedom of association; all of the things that come attached to being a free citizen went completely out of the picture. She knew that there was no freedom guaranteed then, even though her compatriots had the right to vote and participate as in any democracy.

At the time cheating with taxes was a common practice in the capital city where she grew up. Paulina tells us about a lady who earned a living coming to workplaces and selling receipts. Personal income taxes were paid by the earner (not as in the UK's PAYE system where the employer deducts and pays the tax to the HMRC) while this tax system allowed for various deductions. So this lady sold receipts for substantial amounts. The price she took was 5% of the amount stated on the receipts.

> [I]t was like petrol station kind of receipts. These had big, big amounts of money, you know, hundreds and hundreds. Your name was clearly stated on the receipts and people just bought these receipts from her.

Paulina said she bought such receipts but now feels pretty awful about it. But it was something 'everybody' did.

In comparison Paulina knows that working and living in the UK, she pays a lot of taxes. Although they add up to a lot of money, she is fine with it. As she says:

> If we didn't have taxes, if we didn't pay taxes, what would we have as a safety net and as a part of being in this group in this society? You know, it pays for the school and for my kids' medical care which I would have had to pay for in my native country. That is inconceivable for me living here, in this country. Back at home, well that's another story. There I would have to pay for absolutely everything. Although there is a Social Security system and hospitals, everybody says that if you can pay privately, please go private.

Paulina talks about giving birth in the UK. Her mother came over to help her out and was absolutely astonished and immensely happy for them that giving birth at the hospital did not cost anything—even though Paulina had a caesarean section.

There are several takeaways from Paulina's story as a fiscal culture using Hannerz's frames of state, market, movement and consociality. Paulina relates to the state through payment of taxes. She recognises the limits of what her native South American state offered, both in the past and in the present. This comparison of democratic rights—freedoms as she calls them—makes her even more appreciative of those in the UK. This is one of the reasons she more happily pays taxes in the UK. Her views on healthcare are framed both by the market and by the state; here is public healthcare but not of the quality that the private alternative can offer, so there she would have to concede to pay for such services. If she had stayed in her native country and given birth there, she would probably just have had the same expectation and views on this as her mother. In the UK, she knows that the high taxes, by comparison, she pays in the UK goes to, among other things, public healthcare, and she finds it fantastic.

Movement affects both people and ideas. Paulina brought her memories and experiences from her upbringing and related them to her experiences of living in the UK. There, people gathered around the practice of buying fake receipts as an economic protest against the government. She relates to this memory, but as one that probably increases her willingness to pay tax in the UK; she sees that she receives better services and a political system and society she better thrives in. She says:

> You know, I am lucky to be in this country out of choice. I was not a refugee; I'm not here because of economic reasons. I am here because I want to be here and I want my kids to be here. Our family belongs here.

It all comes together in her final point. 'I feel grateful, yes. But it also has to do with taking responsibility for one another. I think migrants who can feel that they are safe here, they are really happy to contribute, to be part of such a system and to give a little'.

Our point is not that she is a statistically relevant example; our point is rather to illustrate how we, migrants or natives, can relate to the concept of fiscal culture. Most importantly, taxes are complex, and in a modern society like the UK, it touches on many aspects of how human life is organised—of our relation to the state, to the market and to other people (the consociality frame). But our views on taxes also change as we learn more about the functioning state and society and how we compare them with other countries; as migrants the comparison between native and adopted country comes easily. Our attitudes and views might be slow to change, but they do change; they move as we move through life and landscapes—time and space. A fiscal culture is thus never static but constantly in motion. The state changes tax laws and collection procedures. Fiscal needs may radically change (e.g. the US weaponising tariffs or the global war-mongering going on with many countries increasing their military capacity which is partly funded by tax). People hold many different views on taxation and government spending that change very slowly, others can be changed abruptly, disagreeing with how tax money is used or being content with welfare services. Immigrating as a grown-up allows you to compare fiscal policies and practices between your native and adopted country. To suggest that an immigrant 'holds' a fiscal culture is just plain wrong!

Reflection

The concept of a fiscal culture offers a more holistic and dynamic understanding of how individuals relate to both paying taxes and receiving public benefits. Moving beyond static categorisations based on nationality or legal status, fiscal culture encapsulates the complex, lived experiences and evolving attitudes people hold towards the fiscal state. Drawing on anthropological insights and building from tax culture literature, the chapter argues that a fiscal culture is shaped through the interplay of four societal frames: the *state* (laws, institutions and public services), the *market* (economic activity and value creation), *movement* (circulating ideas and experiences) and *consociality* (interpersonal networks and everyday social interaction).

Through the ethnographic case of Paulina, a British-South American human rights lawyer, the chapter illustrates how fiscal culture emerges from the convergence of personal histories, institutional trust, moral values and comparative lived experiences. Paulina's narrative demonstrates how trust in the UK's public services and a strong sense of social responsibility contribute to her willingness to pay taxes—despite a past shaped by tax avoidance practices in her native country. Her evolving sense of belonging and civic engagement underlines that fiscal culture is not static or inherently tied to national identity; rather, it is adaptive, emotional and informed by ongoing comparisons and lived realities.

Ultimately, the chapter contends that recognising the nuanced and shifting nature of fiscal culture—especially through the lens of migrants—can deepen our understanding of taxpayer behaviour and inform more inclusive and effective public policy. Fiscal culture is not something one 'holds', but something people live, constantly shaped by their interactions with state institutions, economic practices and societal norms.

References

Appadurai, A. 1996. *Modernity at large: Cultural dimensions of globalization*. University of Minnesota Press.

Atuguba, R. A. 2021. Tax culture: Perspectives from an African state. *American Journal of Trade and Policy* 8 (1): 17–50. https://doi.org/10.18034/ajtp.v8i1.510.

Baskerville, R. F. 2003. Hofstede never studied culture. *Accounting, Organizations and Society* 28 (1): 1–14. https://doi.org/10.1016/S0361-3682(01)00048-4.

Bergman, M. 2003. Tax reforms and tax compliance: The divergent paths of Chile and Argentina. *Journal of Latin American Studies* 35 (3): 593–624. http://journals.cambridge.org/abstract_S0022216X03006850.

Björklund Larsen, L. 2017. *Shaping taxpayers. Values in action at the Swedish tax agency*. Berghahn Books.

Boas, F. 1897. *The social organization and secret societies of the Kawkiutl Indians*. National Museum of Washington.

Boll, K. 2014. Shady car dealings and taxing work practices: An ethnography of a tax audit process. *Accounting, Organizations and Society* 39 (1): 1–19.

Braunstein, Ruth. 2024. Toward a cultural sociology of taxation. *Socio-Economic Review* 22 (2): 931–952. https://doi.org/10.1016/j.poetic.2022.101682.

Closs-Davies, S. C., K. P. R. Bartels, and D. M. Merkl-Davies. 2020. 'The frog in the pan': Relational transformation of public values in the UK tax authority. *Accounting, Auditing and Accountability Journal* 34 (7): 1635–1663. https://doi.org/10.1108/AAAJ-11-2019-4280.

Dahlén, T. 1997. *Among the interculturalists. An emergent profession and its packaging of knowledge*. Stockholm University.

Esping-Andersen, G. 1990. *The three worlds of welfare capitalism*. John Wiley and Sons.

Evans, C. 2017. Editorial: The complex and critical relationship between tax and corruption. *EJournal of Tax* 15 (2): 140–393.

Fabian, J. 1983. *Time and the other: How anthropology makes its object*. Columbia University Press.

Gaber, S., and I. Gruevski. 2018. The influence of tax culture in improving tax compliance. *Journal of Economics* 3 (2): 80–88.

Geertz, C. 1973. *The interpretation of cultures. Selected essays*. Basic Books.

Gribnau, H. 2015. Corporate social responsibility and tax planning not by rules alone. *Social and Legal Studies* 24 (2): 225–250. http://sls.sagepub.com/content/24/2/225.short.

Gunnarsson, Å. 2020. Fair and sustainable taxation—From a European horizon. *Florida Tax Review* 23 (2): 695–712.

Hannerz, U. 1969. *Cultural complexity: Studies in the social organisation of meaning*. Columbia University Press.

Hannerz, U. 1987. The world in creolisation. *Africa: Journal of the International African Institute* 57 (4): 546–559.

Hannerz, U. 2016. *Writing future worlds. An anthropologist explores global scenarios*. Palgrave Macmillan.

Hannerz, U. 2019. *World watching: Streetcorners and newsbeats on a journey through anthropology*. London: Routledge.

Hart, K. 1973. Informal income opportunities and urban employment in Ghana. *The Journal of Modern Africa Studies* 11 (1): 61–89.

Hart, Keith. 2001. Informal Economy. In *International encyclopaedia of social and behavioural sciences*, 845–846. Oxford: Elsevier.

Hofstede, G. 2011. Dimensionalizing cultures: The Hofstede models in context. *Online Readings in Psychology and Culture, Unit* 2 (2): 1–26.

Ingold, T. 1994. *Companion encyclopedia of anthropology. Humanity, culture and social life*. London: Routledge.

Kuandykov, N., Y. Abil, A. Utepov, A. Nurkey, and A. Abenova. 2021. Investigating the relationship between tax culture and tax communication in Kazakhstan. *Problems and Perspectives in Management* 19 (3): 197–210. https://doi.org/10.21511/ppm.19(3).2021.17.

Likhovski, A. 2011. Chasing ghosts: On writing cultural histories of tax law. *UC IRVINE LAW REVIEW* 1 (3): 843–892.

Livingston, M. A. 2005. Law, culture, and anthropology: On the hopes and limits of comparative tax. *Canadian Journal of Law and Jurisprudence* 18 (1): 119–134. https://doi.org/10.1017/s084182090000552x.

Livingston, M. A. 2020. *Tax and culture. Convergence, divergence, and the future of tax law*. Cambridge University Press. https://doi.org/10.1017/9781316480144.

Malinowski, B. (1922a). *Argonauts of the Western Pacific. An account of native enterprise and adventure in the Archipelagoes of Melanesian Guinea*. https://scholar.google.se/scholar?hl=sv&q=malinowski+1922&btnG=#5

Malinowski, B. 1922b. Ethnology and the study of society. *Economica* 6:208–219.

Mumford, A. 2002. *Taxing culture. Towards a theory of tax collection law*. Routledge.

Nerrè, B. 2008. Tax culture: A basic concept for tax politics. *Economic Analysis and Policy* 38 (1): 153–167. https://doi.org/10.1016/S0313-5926(08)50011-7.

OECD (Organisation for Co-operation and Development). (2015 [2021]). *Building tax culture, compliance and citizenship*. https://doi.org/10.1787/9789264205154-en.

Ordower, H. 2010. The culture of tax avoidance. *Saint Louis University Law Journal* 55 (1): 47–128. https://doi.org/10.2139/ssrn.1596684.

Rawlings, G. 2003. Contesting fairness and fragmenting groups: Cultural narratives of taxation and citizenship in globalising Australia. *Australian Journal of Social Issues* 38 (3): 269–298. https://doi.org/10.1002/j.1839-4655.2003.tb01147.x.

Saleheen, A. M. 2013. The use of discretions in taxation: The case of VAT in Bangladesh. *eJournal of Tax Research* 11 (1): 97–113.

Sánchez Román, J. A. 2013. Resistance without revolt: Shaping a tax culture in modern Argentina, 1930–1955. *Journal of Policy History* 25 (3): 422–443. https://doi.org/10.1017/S0898030613000183.

Smircich, L. 1983. Concepts of culture and organizational analysis. *Administrative Science Quarterly* 28 (3): 339. https://doi.org/10.2307/2392246.

Steinmo, S. H. 2018. *The leap of faith. The fiscal foundations of successful government in Europe and America*. Oxford University Press.

Tylor, E. 1871. *Primitive culture: Researches into the development of mythology, philosophy, religion, art and custom*. Murray.

CHAPTER 7

Some Final Thoughts

Abstract In this concluding chapter we provide some insights into what our approach to the topography of taxation may provide but also look into the unforeseeable future. What will it bring? We know about generative AI, climate change, demographic changes, and geopolitical upheaval, including emerging trade wars precipitated by tax in the form of tariffs, but there might even be black swans in our landscape. This book has provided a critical yet holistic perspective that we hope inspires research into how people and society will react to new taxes and ways to tax.

Keywords Critical perspective • Fiscal belonging • Thin and thick reciprocity • Fiscal culture • Future research on tax

> Paths are the habits of a landscape. They are acts of consensual making.
> —Robert Macfarlane in *The Old Ways: A Journey on Foot*

Wandering through the tax landscape as a newcomer may be a bewildering experience. You might encounter beautiful foliage, rolling meadows or opulent fields; sand dunes or craggy rocks; mountains and valleys, well-walked paths or asphalted roads with signs directing you here, there and everywhere. Some aspects of the landscape can be recognisable from walk-abouts in the past; others are totally new and have to be made sense of.

Walking through a landscape can also be a very familiar experience. On the everyday walk with the dog, you know the turns and twists of the path,

L. Björklund Larsen, L. Oats, *Crossing Borders, Sharing Burdens*,
https://doi.org/10.1007/978-3-031-99394-7_7

the view that opens up once passing the crest and there is no need to read the signs. But lo and behold, one day some things might have changed. A storm damaging some trees, a new path made by the municipality, a fence put up, sheltering you from the wind or obstructing the view.

We are fascinated by how tax knowledge is produced, and as a starting point for this book, we wanted to illustrate what tax knowledge consists of and what premises underlie it, but also who has created such knowledge and how. To address this aim we have illustrated one form of tax knowledge, which generated in the world of academic disciplines, with the topography of a landscape. This allows us to focus on different aspects of tax, not excluding the importance of one over another. The topography of tax is a reminder that knowledge of tax is varied and always partial. Acknowledging this, and following our own critical path, also allows us to better understand how migrants relate to paying tax, knowing that they also recognise, and in the best of worlds, the benefits of taxation. This is what we refer to as fiscal belonging.

There are four takeaways from trekking through this book. First, a brief glimpse of some social theories and what they are capable of revealing when applying a critical perspective on tax. Second, we present fiscal belonging as a way to understand the very human need for making sense of our place in relation to other people as we pay taxes and benefit from them. Third, we introduce the concept of thin and thick reciprocity as a way of nuancing the various facets of fiscal belonging in which people engage. Fourth, we take an encompassing perspective looking into what thinking with the concept of fiscal culture provides.

Critical Perspective

Just recognising the existence of different forms of knowledge can lead to a critical perspective on taxation; perhaps some tax scholars will find the metaphor of topography challenging. Yet this is also our aim. We are very serious about the societal importance of taxation; as it affects many, many aspects of private and social life, we issue a call to arms for all resources possible to address the issue. In a rapidly changing world, we cannot leave unchallenged the dominance of entrenched ways of thinking about tax.

We have briefly introduced a few social theories to help illustrate how migrants to the UK relate to tax and being taxed. Fiscal citizenship is a concept that describes in various ways the relation between taxpayers and the nation in which they reside. The relation can be political, reciprocal, distinguishing between different types of taxes or redistributional or invoke the notion of a social contract. There are many insights to be learnt from studies of 'fiscal citizenship', yet our main objections to using it are twofold. First, the term seems to be mainly coined by American scholarship, perhaps given the US tax code obligating all citizens to declare their taxable income and resources.[1] Second, and more importantly, our participants seldom related taxes to citizenship. Instead we draw on the scholarship of belonging, especially inspired by Nira Yuval-Davis' proposed facets. Her facets are multiple, interrelated, non-hierarchical and subject to change; all are pertinent to our field.

We use a loose formulation of field theory to describe the UK context. The notion of 'a field' seems to fit nicely into our topography metaphor. Our 'field' is the UK fiscal field, within which migrants must engage with complex bureaucracies administering broader public policies. We describe the context of UK tax law, organisation of taxation and immigration, as well as a few critical incidents that have created controversies and challenged how we understand the field(s). How migrants engage with the UK fiscal field depends on how comfortable they feel in the fiscal field and how this is coloured by their experiences in the immigration field.

A third perspective is the more holistic 'culture'. Here we draw on anthropological research of cultures, the discipline where culture is one of the most central concepts. Tax scholars from many disciplines have taken a stab at tax in terms of fiscal culture, yet few are based on ethnographic research giving voice to people in 'the field'. A culture consists of learnt and shared beliefs and behaviours, which we exemplified by Paulina's narrative. Interpreting her story as fiscal culture draws on the interplay between Ulf Hannerz's organisational frames of state, market, movement and consociality. It provides a more holistic and dynamic understanding of what a fiscal culture may be relating to both paying taxes and receiving public benefits. Paulina's evolving sense of belonging and civic engagement underlines that fiscal culture is not static or inherently tied to national identity; rather, it is adaptive, emotional and informed by ongoing comparisons and lived realities.

[1] The USA being only one of two countries in the world that requires all citizens to declare taxable income and wealth.

Fiscal Belonging

The term 'fiscal citizenship' is often invoked without any clear explanation of what it means. Although meaningful analytically, it was not a concept referred to when we spoke to our participants. Without explicitly referring to the term fiscal citizenship, they became hesitant about the connection between citizenship and fiscal contribution and engagement, focusing largely on the formalities of citizenship. What came through was that a sense of belonging is more important to them than formal citizenship when it comes to taxes. This was explicitly articulated for European migrants as Brexit happened; their automatic work permit ended and they needed to apply for British citizenship in order to stay on and work.

When our participants spoke about belonging according to social categories, it was with reference to employment, wealth, level of education, being a parent but also about race. The oft-applied social categories of class and gender did not seem to make much of a difference for the various facets of fiscal belonging. There were however some references to the ultra-rich 1%, but this group of people was more likely referred to as a hazy imaginary on the horizon. No one knew anyone belonging to this group; their engagement with these was mostly based on hearsay and media reporting. Instead of class and gender, the right to work, a job and proper employment were stronger for belonging. It is not only that they create financial security, but they give access to insurance, pensions and other socio-economic institutions as well as engaging with colleagues. Work is thus one facet of fiscal belonging. The second is family. Having a partner and especially children creates longer-term commitment—and a sense of belonging—to the adopted country; they will be raised, educated and possibly live here. The third facet is social acceptance—to be able to connect to people, make friendships, be addressed by strangers in the same manner as everybody else and be treated with respect by authorities. Race was notably an obstacle here; in particular, men with darker skin colour felt less socially accepted. The final facet we propose is values which include both cultural and political values. This concerns how the adopted country is governed and functions. What premises underly the relationship between public institutions and the people they serve—or govern for that matter. What are public views and practices on transparency, predictability and corruption? Can these institutions be trusted to collect and use tax in an equitable way?

Following Yuval-Davis' lead, our four facets are neither hierarchical nor exclusionary, are subject to change as society, including tax laws and policies, and are continuously up for negotiation. Yet, although the facets exist on the same level, there were nuances in how our participants related to them.

Thin and Thick Reciprocity

Virtually all taxpayers resonate with the idea of getting 'something for your money'. By unpacking the different facets of belonging, and overlaying them with thin and thick reciprocity, we get a stronger sense of willingness to contribute financially to the society in which we live. This is closely connected to the degrees of belongingness that vary over time. Thin reciprocity is more transactional and can be seen as tit-for-tat reasoning. It comes close to benefit theory. The layer of thin reciprocity leads to estimates of how much I, as a taxpayer, contribute in relation to others, but also—noting the fiscal component—is perceived to benefit from my tax payments. Thin reciprocity may be personal but can also relate to other individuals or other categories in society. It is to a large extent a perception game of who is seen to contribute and who benefits from such contributions. Thick reciprocity is more encompassing, with an affectionate view on sharing and a deep understanding of what taxes contribute to society. There is recognition of the economic contribution and transactional view on taxes, but more importantly that taxes have made possible a society in which values resonate with my own. Fiscal contribution flavoured by thick reciprocity is a way to give back, invest in the future and contribute to the social fabric.

Adding thick and thin reciprocity to our sense of belonging makes it possible to bring nuance to our facets. In particular it makes for a useful distinction between the transactional (thin) and more emotional/affective (thick) ways of reciprocating.

Fiscal Culture

The case of Paulina, the human rights lawyer born in South America, illustrates how the concept of fiscal culture may offer a more holistic but also dynamic understanding of how individuals relate to both paying taxes and receiving public benefits. Moving beyond static categorisations based on nationality or legal status, fiscal culture encapsulates the complex, lived experiences and evolving attitudes people hold towards the fiscal state. What it means to be a human being paying tax and recognising the benefits tax provides. Drawing on anthropological insights and building from tax culture literature, we illustrate how a fiscal culture can be shaped through the interplay of four societal frames. The *state* is made up of laws, institutions and public services. The *market* consists of all economic activity and the value that is created through such exchanges. *Movement* concerns the circulating of ideas and experiences, within and beyond borders. Finally, *consociality* encompasses interpersonal networks and everyday social interaction with family, friends, neighbours and other people that cross one's way.

A fiscal culture thus emerges from the convergence of personal histories, institutional trust, moral values and comparative lived experiences. Paulina's narrative demonstrates how trust in the UK's public services and a strong sense of social responsibility contribute to her willingness to pay taxes—despite a past shaped by tax avoidance practices in her native country. Her evolving sense of belonging and civic engagement underlines that fiscal culture is not static or inherently tied to national identity. As we see from Paulina's story, a fiscal culture emerges as adaptive, emotional and informed by ongoing comparisons and lived realities.

Recognising the nuanced and shifting nature of fiscal culture—especially through the lens of migrants—can deepen our understanding of taxpayer behaviour and inform more inclusive and effective public policy. Fiscal culture is not something one 'holds', but something people live. It is constantly shaped by interactions with state institutions, economic practices and societal norms.

Possibilities for the Future

Although we draw on roundtables and interviews of well-educated migrants to the UK, a quite specific group of people, we suggest that there are lessons to be learnt for a broader audience. Thinking with fiscal belonging, how is it articulated among natives, youngsters or other categories of taxpayer? In Ghana, Guatemala or Greece? And what can we learn from applying such a perspective?

Our results also lead us to speculate whether some tax research has actually looked at the wrong variables? Has the focus on quantifying morals, social norms and attitudes got it wrong when aiming to understand why people pay tax? We would propose a further investigation into how feelings of belonging and reciprocity are the main drivers for people's willingness to contribute. If so, this might have far-reaching implications for tax policy, not least taking some of the load away from tax collectors and moving the focus to politicians spending tax revenue on issues people approve of.

We currently live in a rapid-changing world where public responses might have a profound impact on taxation. What most thought of as living with a world order with well-defined organisational structures and firm international relations is quickly changing. Discussions about defence have dwarfed previous worries about climate change. Digitalisation and AI transform work and thus also sources of tax. Public responses to these serious challenges will have important economic and societal implications. We not only foresee an increased focus on taxation to finance all of this but are also intrigued by how such changes in taxation will affect society, the people living in it and their relations. In the landscape of taxation forests might be ravaged, paths and roads relocated; there might even be serious changes similar to earthquakes. To understand this, a more holistic focus of the fiscal belonging concept might prove helpful.

Our hope is that this book will provide inspiration, and even lay down a challenge, to scholars both new and established, not only tax scholars but also those interested in public policy. We hope to have shown that tax, both collecting and spending, is immensely interesting and complex and affects both individuals and society in many ways. Be curious, be courageous and explore this wonderful landscape we have sketched in this book.

Index[1]

[1] Note: Page numbers followed by 'n' refer to notes.

L. Björklund Larsen, L. Oats, *Fiscal Belonging*,
https://doi.org/10.1007/978-3-031-99394-7

Kolibri 360 GmbH
Ferdinand-Jühlke-Straße 7
99095 Erfurt, Deutschland
produktsicherheit@kolibri360.de